KALASHNIKOV AK47 SERIES

THE 7.62 × 39MM ASSAULT RIFLE IN DETAIL

KALASHNIKOV AK47 SERIES

THE 7.62 × 39MM ASSAULT RIFLE IN DETAIL

MARTIN J. BRAYLEY

THE CROWOOD PRESS

First published in 2013 by
The Crowood Press Ltd
Ramsbury, Marlborough
Wiltshire SN8 2HR

www.crowood.com

British Library Cataloguing-in-Publication Data
A catalogue record for this book is available from the British Library.

ISBN 978 1 84797 483 9

Acknowledgements
The author would like to acknowledge the following for providing assistance with the production of this book: Toby Brayley, UK; Paul Paxton, UK; John James, UK; WO Ed Storey, Canadian Military Engineers; Terry Moon, USA; Janette Palubicki, UK; Media Image Photography, UK; PDH Enterprises, UK; Antiques Storehouse, UK; AJS Militaria, UK; Hampshire Constabulary, UK; United States Department of Defense; Hungarian Defence Ministry; ISAF Media; Republic of Serbia Ministry of Defence.

Author's note
As the title suggests this book explores the variety of weapon types loosely termed Kalashnikov or AK47 by the masses and the media. This is undoubtedly the most readily recognized weapon type ever produced. However, the generic terms Kalashnikov and AK47 cover a vast number of weapon variants and national production far beyond the original design by Mikhail Timofeyevich Kalashnikov. This book sets out to detail the principal design features of the Avtomat Kalashnikov series of weapons using the original 7.62×39mm M1943 cartridge and the licensed and illegal variants produced worldwide.

The official Soviet designation of 7.62mm Avtomat Kalashnikov obrazets 1947g was usually abbreviated to 7.62mm AK, with the same designation being applied to the first three variants of the weapon (types 1, 2 and 3 receivers). In the West the incorrect, but generally accepted, designation of the weapon type is AK47. In an effort to provide the correct national designations, however, the term AK has been used throughout this work to apply to the first three variants of the AK rifle. The Soviet designation for the fourth pattern stamped steel receiver was Avtomat Kalashnikov Modernizirovanniy, abbreviated to AKM, and again the official designation is used in this work.

At the time of the AK47's development the country now known as Russia formed part of the Union of Soviet Socialist Republics or Soviet Union. Similarly, references to Yugoslavia cover events before 2003, while references to Serbia cover those after that date or weapons that may be identified with Serbian forces.

Designed and typeset by Guy Croton

Printed and bound in India by Replika Press Pvt Ltd

Contents

Introduction

The Great Patriotic War

At the turn of the twentieth century the standard Russian infantry weapon was the 7.62×54mm M1891 Mosin Nagant rifle. This rifle was typical for the period. Wooden stocked, it fired a smokeless cartridge from a five-round integral magazine and had sights graduated in Arshin (a measurement equivalent to 71.12cm/28in). The M1891 bayonet issued with the rifle was a somewhat obsolete design. At a time when the majority of the world's armies were using knife or sword type bayonets, the Russians introduced a cruciform section socket bayonet that was to be carried fitted to the rifle at all times and was therefore not provided with a scabbard.

The rifle was modified in 1930 to the M1891/30. The minor improvements included a hooded foresight post, reducing the barrel length by 9cm (3.5in) and marking the sight graduation in metres.

In 1938 a short version of the M1891/30 rifle was introduced into service as the M1938 carbine. Essentially little more than an M1891/30 rifle with a reduced barrel length, giving an overall length some 20cm (8in) shorter than the rifle, the carbine was designed for rear echelon troops. It had no provision for the attachment of a bayonet, an unnecessary expense for troops who were unlikely to engage an enemy at bayonet point. However, the experiences of the Great Patriotic War suggested differently and it was soon realized that even rear echelon troops would benefit from having a bayonet. The M1938 carbine was thus modified in 1943 by the provision of a folding spike bayonet permanently fitted at the muzzle. The modified carbine with bayonet entered service as the M1944 carbine, which was to see extensive post-war service with many Soviet satellites and politically allied nations.

While the majority of Russian troops were armed with bolt action rifles, the interwar years saw extensive research into self-loading and fully automatic rifles. A modified self-loading version of the 1891 rifle had been made in 1910 by Fedor Tokarev but it was not taken into service. During the early 1930s Sergei Simonov undertook work that resulted in the adoption in 1936 of the gas-operated Avtomaticheskaya Vintovka Simonova AVS36 rifle. The design was to prove unsatisfactory, however, and production was terminated in 1938 when a Tokarev design was accepted into service. The Samozaryadnaya Vintovka Tokareva SVT38 was an improvement over the AVS36, but it too was not without its problems and was not well received by the troops using it. Therefore in 1940 a modified and improved version was introduced into service as the SVT40. The 7.62×54mm rimmed cartridge had been used in the AVS and SVT rifles, but at best it was unsuited to gas-operated weapons' magazine feed and it

Tank Corps Stárshiy Serzhánt (Senior Sergeant) Mikhail Timofeyevich Kalashnikov photographed at his drawing board during the Great Patriotic War. Kalashnikov began studying weapon design during a period of convalescence after being wounded during the battle of Bryansk in October 1941 when he was serving as the commander of a T34 tank of the 24th Tank Regiment. Private collection

Russia adopted the bolt-action Mosin Nagant rifle in 1891. Shown above is the slightly modified version of the M1891, the M1891/30 rifle, the mainstay of Soviet infantry weapons during World War II. Below is the Tokarev SVT40, a gas-operated self-loading rifle that had originally been intended to replace the M1891 rifle in Russian service. The outbreak of war and design problems with the SVT rifles resulted in the bolt-action M1891s remaining standard, but with a third of infantry troops supposedly armed with the SVT40. The M1891 rifle was fitted with a quadrangular-bladed socket bayonet but there was no provision for a scabbard as it was intended to be carried on the weapon at all times. The SVT M1940 was provided with a knife bayonet carried on the belt in a steel scabbard. Media Image Photography

The M1891 rifles were excessively long for many users, so a carbine version was produced for rear echelon troops. Above is the Mosin Nagant M1938 carbine. Essentially a shortened M1891/30 rifle, it had no provision for attaching a bayonet. Below is the M1944 carbine, merely an M1938 carbine fitted with a permanently attached folding bayonet. As with many Soviet weapons, the M1944 carbines were produced by other communist nations; at bottom is a Chinese copy, the Type 53 carbine. Media Image Photography

Russian sub machine guns were essential tools in Soviet infantry doctrine and were to prove invaluable in the close-quarter battles typified by the actions fought in Stalingrad and Leningrad. Above is the ubiquitous PPSh M1941 shown with the 35-round box magazine and the 71-round drum magazine that were issued with the weapon. The drum magazine was the more popular of the two. Below is the PPS M1943, which was introduced as a lighter and cheaper alternative to the PPSh. The PPS was only provided with a 35-round box magazine. Media Image Photography

The SKS M1945 carbine was originally conceived in 1943 and used the new 7.62×39mm 'intermediate' cartridge. It had an integral 10-round magazine and a permanently attached folding knife bayonet. The SKS was short lived as it was soon made obsolete by the Kalashnikov. Above is a Soviet-made SKS, below is the Yugoslav M1959/66 with integral grenade launcher (the M1959 version had no grenade launcher) and at bottom is the Chinese version, the Type 56 carbine (not to be confused with the Type 56 rifle). Media Image Photography

was undoubtedly overpowered. It had been anticipated that a self-loading weapon would eventually replace all bolt action rifles in Soviet service, with early war Soviet tables of organization and equipment showing a scale of 33 per cent of infantry rifles supposedly being self-loading. This figure was not achieved as the gas-operated rifle was expensive and time-consuming to manufacture. Thus production of the SVT40 declined in favour of simpler bolt action rifles and sub machine guns (SMG) as the Great Patriotic War progressed.

While the rifle was the standard infantry arm of all nation's armies, the close-quarter fighting experienced in the dense forests of Finland during the 'Winter War' showed that the powerful 7.62×54mm cartridge was over-ranged and a long bayonet was often unwieldy, with the M1891 rifle not being best suited to that type of warfare. Indeed, the SMG was an ideal weapon for such combat. Having a high rate of fire, large magazine capacity and a lighter cartridge with a shorter effective range (150m/500ft for an SMG against 500m/1,600ft for the M1891/30), the SMG was ideal for fighting in dense woodland or urban areas where visibility was greatly reduced by obstructions and contact ranges were therefore close. The Pistolet-Pulemyot Degtyaryova (PPD) SMG was in limited service with Russian forces as the PPD34, PPD34/38 and PPD40 variants but it was expensive to produce and had not been issued in great numbers. The PPD had proved highly effective in the invasion of Poland and the 'Winter War' against Finland. Although the PPD was expensive and time-consuming to produce, it did provide the inspiration for an SMG designed by Georgi Shpagin, the Pistolet-Pulemyot Shpagina (PPSh41). The

PPSh41 used the same 7.62×25mm cartridge as the PPD but was simpler and cheaper to produce, using fewer parts and taking almost half the manufacturing time. The PPSh41 was a selective fire weapon with a heavy wooden stock. It could be used with a 35-round box magazine or a 71-round drum magazine, providing the infantryman with excellent close-range firepower. However, Operation *Barbarossa*, Hitler's surprise invasion of the Soviet Union in June 1941, rapidly led to severe pressure on Soviet manufacturing plants with a spiralling demand for armaments of all types. The drain on resources was immense. Although some six million PPSh41s were made during World War II, the Soviets needed an even simpler and cheaper SMG. The requirement was met by the Pistolet-Pulemjot Sudaeva PPS, designed by Alexei Sudayev. The PPS was an ideal design for mass production with little use of machining and a reliance on sheet steel stampings. It used the standard 7.62×25mm cartridge, the wooden stock was discarded in favour of a folding steel skeleton pattern and it used only half of the steel required for the PPSh41. Machining time was reduced to a little over 2.7 hours compared to 7.3 hours for the PPSh41 or 13.7 for the PPD40. Added to this, the reduction in the number of labourers required and the overall labour time provided for a theoretically massive increase in output. The PPS was originally adopted as the PPS42, but manufacturing refinements and even further simplification of the weapon led to it being re-designated the PPS43 in 1943. The PPS43 could only be fired full automatic and was only provided with a 35-round box magazine with no provision for a drum magazine. More than two million PPS43s were manufactured during World War II.

Kurdish Peshmerga fighters pose with a Russian AKS and an AMD65 in northern Iraq in 1991. The fighters' magazines are carried in individual leather pockets on US-supplied webbing belts (this type of magazine pouch is shown in detail in the Iraqi section on page 75). While serving with 3 Commando Brigade in Iraq during 1991 the author observed a variety of Kalashnikov type weapons in use with the Peshmerga, including examples of Russian, Hungarian and Chinese manufacture. Author's photograph

A young Nicaraguan army soldier cleans his AKMS rifle, 1999. The magazine, bolt carrier and recoil spring are at bottom left, with the receiver cover at lower right. The Kalashnikov is a simple weapon and can easily be field stripped and maintained with little training. Author's photograph

A US Army Sergeant First Class instructs Iberian soldiers on the use of the Kalashnikov rifle. The Romanian-made PM md 63 is well used and in need of some basic maintenance. The special tool used to provide lateral adjustment of the foresight is laid on the sandbag just below the weapon's handguard. Vertical adjustment of the foresight is undertaken with the combination tool. US Department of Defense

While lacking power, the 7.62×25mm cartridge was excellent for close range combat and the 7.62×54mm was equally good for long range use in rifles or sustained fire weapons (such as the M1910 Maxim or DP machine guns). The Soviets had realized that neither was an ideal calibre for modern warfare, with ranges of engagement rarely over 300m (1,000ft), and that some form of cartridge was required to bridge the gap. Weapon designers had therefore worked towards developing an intermediate round that would provide for improved range and accuracy over the 7.62×25mm but without the excessive range and power of the 7.62×54mm cartridge. The result was the 7.62×39mm M1943 intermediate round, which had evolved from an experimental 7.62×41mm cartridge. The new 7.62×39mm cartridge was perfect for medium range use. It had a tapered case providing for easy extraction and, unlike the 7.62×54mm round, it was rimless, which dramatically improved its performance in magazine-fed weapons. One of the first weapons to be built for the new cartridge was developed by Sergei Gavrilovich Simonov. Simonov's weapon, similar to the AVS36 in general appearance but with a fixed magazine and integral folding bayonet, was originally designed for the 7.62×54mm ammunition but modified for the new M1943 intermediate round. The Samozaryadnyj Karabin sistemy Simonova (SKS) first saw limited field testing of pre-production rifles in 1944 where it proved reliable and popular with the troops using it. The following year it was accepted into service as the Samozaryadnyj Karabin Simonova 45. The SKS was not put into full production until 1949, by which time a new weapon had already attracted the attention of the Soviet hierarchy, a weapon that would make all other Soviet rifles obsolete.

Sgt Kalashnikov and the Birth of the AK Rifle

Mikhail Timofeyevich Kalashnikov had been conscripted into the Red Army in 1938. He was trained as a tank driver/mechanic and soon rose to the rank of Stárshiy Serzhánt (Senior Sergeant) with command of a T34 tank of the 24th Tank Regiment, 12th Tank Division. He saw action with his regiment, including at the battle of Brody in June 1941. During the battle of Bryansk in October 1941 the Soviets were defeated and the town of Bryansk was almost completely destroyed with some 80,000 killed. It was during this battle that the twenty-one-year-old Kalashnikov was wounded, receiving shrapnel injuries to his chest and shoulder, but he was able to make his own way to a field hospital. His wounds led to an extended period of recuperation away from the fighting. It was during this time, and against a backdrop of what would now possibly be diagnosed as a form of 'stress disorder', that Kalashnikov developed an obsessive desire to create a weapon capable of driving the German invaders from his motherland. At this time Kalashnikov would probably not have been aware of the development of the PPSh41, but he would undoubtedly have been familiar with the bolt action M1891 and perhaps also the AVS and SVT rifles, as well as the unreliability of these later two gas-operated weapons. It was during his convalescence that Kalashnikov designed and, with the approval and assistance of his former employer at the Turkistan-Siberian railway yards, built a sub machine gun. This weapon was considered unsuitable for adoption but Kalashnikov's weapon design skills were recognized and he was posted to the Artillery Directorate of the Red Army, where he was given every

A US soldier conducts training with Afghan National Police officers. The ANP soldier uses a blue plastic AKM dummy weapon employed for tactical training where live firing is not required or when the use of real weapons may prove unwarranted. US Department of Defense

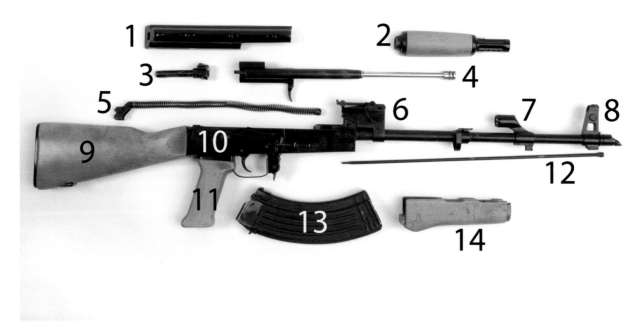

A Hungarian AK63F (AKM) field stripped to show the principal component parts: (1) receiver cover; (2) gas tube and integral gas tube handguard; (3) bolt; (4) bolt carrier and gas piston; (5) recoil spring and recoil spring guide; (6) rear sight and sight block; (7) gas block and bayonet lug; (8) foresight (front sight) block and muzzle brake; (9) stock; (10) receiver and selector lever; (11) pistol grip; (12) cleaning rod; (13) magazine; (14) fore-end (lower handguard). Weapon courtesy Hampshire Constabulary

Detail of a Hungarian AK63F's bolt
carrier: (top) integral white metal piston;
(centre) bolt; (bottom) recoil spring guide
and recoil spring. Weapon courtesy
Hampshire Constabulary

Typical 7.62×39mm steel bodied magazines as used on Kalashnikov rifles. At left are the 75-round drum magazine and 40-round box
magazine designed for use with the RPK squad light machine gun. Both types function readily on AK rifles and are popular with insurgents
and irregular forces. Centre is a standard 30-round Russian-made magazine, a Hungarian 20-round magazine, Yugoslav 15-round magazine
(top) and a Polish 10-round magazine for grenade launching ammunition (below). The 10-round magazine has a restrictor plate fitted
internally at the forward edge, reducing the internal length and preventing the loading of ball or other bulleted ammunition. Only the
special grenade-launching rounds (similar to blank ammunition) can be loaded into this magazine for use with muzzle-launched grenades.
Media Image Photography

encouragement and assistance in refining his skills and his
weapon's design. Despite his efforts with this design and
others, his weapons were not accepted for service, partly
due to the success of the PPSh41. Kalashnikov was not
deterred and continued to work on his ideas and to learn
from other designers and weapon types. Like other
designers, the experimental 7.62×41mm and later the
adopted 7.62×39mm cartridges were focal points for his
weapons designs. After its adoption all new self-loading
rifles were required to function and be fully compatible
with the new intermediate cartridge. Eventually, in 1946,
Kalashnikov fielded a weapon that set the standard. The
Experimental Assault Rifle Number 1 (sometimes called
the AK46) had an unmistakable appearance, a form that
was to become instantly recognizable throughout the
world as a Kalashnikov rifle. It was this weapon, with a few
refinements, that in 1947 was to be accepted into service
with the Soviet army as the 7.62mm Avtomat Kalashnikov
obrazets 1947g, more commonly known as the Avtomat
Kalashnikov or AK. The first production weapons left the
factory the following year with full production
commencing in 1949. However, as with any new weapon,

it was some time before sufficient stocks had been
manufactured to provide for a widespread issue.
Meanwhile the SKS served as the primary Soviet rifle,
although stocks of Mosin Nagant rifles and PPSh SMGs
dominated infantry small arms issue.

The Western powers undoubtedly missed the
introduction of the AK, or if they were aware of its
existence it was kept very secret. It was during the
Hungarian Revolution of 1956 that the world was
introduced to the Avtomat Kalashnikov obrazets 1947g
rifle. Soviet troops sent to quell the uprising carried the
new weapon that had previously been kept from Western
eyes. The Kalashnikov made its world debut and it was
eventually to become probably the most widely recognized
firearm of all time.

The AK has become synonymous with armed struggle
and revolution. The weapon in a stylized form is displayed
on the Mozambique national flag and also appears on the
flags of Hezbollah and the Iranian Revolutionary Guards.
It is a weapon that has appeared in most conflicts of the
last sixty years and will undoubtedly continue to arm
soldiers and revolutionaries for many decades to come.

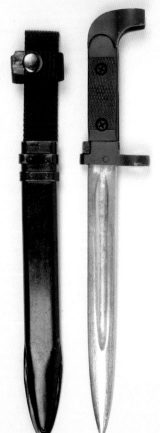

Kalashnikov combination tools:

(top) An Iraqi Tabuk rifle with second pattern combination tool cap fitted over the muzzle nut as a cleaning rod guide. The combination tool body has been fitted to the cleaning rod and is held in place by inserting the screwdriver blade into the body.

(Below) Early pattern combination tool issued with the AK, comprising: (from left to right) combination tool body and cap (requiring the removal of the muzzle nut to use the cap as a bore guide); bristle brush and jag (both fitting to the cleaning rod), and the combined screwdriver/drift/sight adjustment tool. At right is the second pattern combination tool issued with the AKM, comprising: combination tool body and cap (the cap fitted over the muzzle brake to act as a bore guide); bristle brush; jag and loop; drift; screwdriver/sight adjustment tool (the small recess at the side of the screwdriver was used to tighten the jag or brush onto the cleaning rod); and a tapered pin, used in the disassembly of the trigger group.

The combination tool body had numerous openings. These served a number of purposes, including the use of the tool as a handle for the screwdriver/sight adjustment tool using the upper slot visible on the early tool at left. The lower, smaller slot was used to rotate the gas tube lock to release the gas tube handguard. The large opening visible on the later pattern tool at right was used to insert the cleaning rod. Media Image Photography

While Indonesia did not manufacture Kalshnikovs, it did produce a bayonet for imported AK rifles. The Indonesian AK bayonet has chequered black plastic grips (scales) and a black hanger. With the exception of the blade, which remains bright, all metal surfaces are painted black. Overall finish is quite poor compared to Russian bayonets. Media Image Photography

Kalashnikov muzzle fittings: (top left) blank firing adapters (BFAs) for use with blank ammunition, restricting the loss of gases from the muzzle and allowing the weapon action to recycle; (top right) AKM muzzle brakes used to reduce muzzle climb in full automatic fire; (lower left) AK muzzle nut; and (lower right) an East German waterproof rubber muzzle cap. Media Image Photography

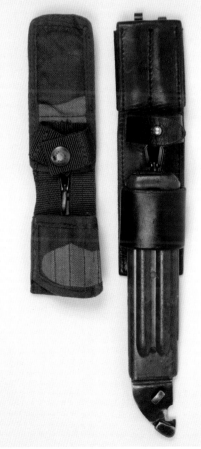

In addition to Romania, the Lithuanians also used bayonet frogs with Russian-made AKM II bayonets. The scabbard was held by a loop that enclosed the throat of the scabbard and small carbine hook that snapped onto the hanger bar. Shown here are a woodland camouflaged bayonet frog at left (also produced in desert camouflage) and a black leather frog with Russian scabbard fitted. The webbing frog has a British PLCE type attachment at the rear, while the leather frog has twin American M1956 pattern clips for suspension. Media Image Photography

US Marines destroy weapons removed from the Iraqi armoury in Al Kut during Operation *Iraqi Freedom* in April 2003. The weapons were burnt and crushed beneath tracked vehicles. A row of weapons is being laid out in the centre of the image ready for crushing while others burn with the aid of gasoline. A variety of AK types are evident, as is a vintage SMLE rifle. US Department of Defense

Kalashnikov Receiver Types

The first receiver made for the Avtomat Kalashnikova (AK) rifle was made from a sheet steel stamping fitted with a machined steel trunnion into which the breech of the barrel was fitted. Problems were encountered with the welding of internal components of the type 1 receiver, including the guide and ejector rails, as the heat generated caused the receiver to warp. This resulted in high levels of component rejection and increased costs. The problems were not easy to rectify and thus work was undertaken to find an alternative method of production. This type was only in production between 1948 and 1951.

The second pattern of receiver used with the AK rifle,

the type 2, reverted to the tried and tested production method of machining the receiver from a solid block of steel. Although costing more and requiring increased labour and time to produce, this machining method resulted in far fewer rejections and a stronger, albeit heavier, end product. The machined steel block receiver was somewhat heavier than the stamped version. To reduce the weight without compromising function or strength, machined cuts were placed on either side of the receiver above the magazine well. The cuts ran parallel with the bore axis.

Typically in weapon development many stages are needed to find the perfect weapon and again the type 2 receiver was not without its own problems. The fitting of

Different Receiver Types		
Receiver type 1A	Stamped receiver, fixed stock	AK (AK47)
Receiver type 1B	Stamped receiver, folding stock	AKS (AKS47)
Receiver type 2A	Machined/forged receiver, fixed stock	AK (AK47)
Receiver type 2B	Machined/forged receiver, folding stock	AKS (AKS47)
Receiver type 3A	Machined/forged receiver, fixed stock	AK (AK47)
Receiver type 3B	Machined/forged receiver, folding stock	AKS (AKS47)
Receiver type 4A	Stamped receiver, fixed stock	AKM
Receiver type 4B	Stamped receiver, folding stock	AKMS

the wooden stock into the type 2A receiver proved to be a weak point. Some basic attention to the issues and a little redesign work resulted in the type 3 receiver.

The type 3 receiver differed from the type 2 mainly in the method of fixing the stock to the receiver. Less obviously, the machined cut-out on both sides of the receiver above the magazine well was orientated parallel to the lower edge of the receiver, providing a distinctly recognizable feature to differentiate the type 3 from the type 2 receiver, which had the cuts parallel with the bore axis.

The problems associated with the type 1 stamped receiver had not been forgotten and some effort was spent attempting to solve the issues in order to field a lighter and simpler weapon. Machined receivers are heavy and stamped receivers have many advantages, not least for the soldiers who have to carry them, since they are about a third lighter: typically the lighter the weapon, the more ammunition could be carried. The problems of the type 1 stamped receivers warping were eventually overcome with simple changes to the design and production methods, with much being learned from German weapons engineers 'working' in Russia. These changes included less use of welding and increased use of riveting and stamped parts where possible, although the weapon still required a forged barrel trunnion and a forged rear trunnion to hold the butt in place. These improvements resulted in the type 4 stamped receiver, and a new weapon designation – the Avtomat Kalashnikova Modernizirovanniy or AKM. The type 4 receiver first appeared during 1955, but it was not until 1959 that the design had been sufficiently developed for it to be accepted into service as the standard weapon type.

Summary of 7.62×39mm Kalashnikov Receiver Types
The designations listed opposite left on page 16 are used to differentiate between the different methods of production of Kalashnikov receivers, and of fixed or folding stocks. They are not official military terminology. Throughout the text, where a suffix is used, type A refers to a fixed stock weapon and type B the folding stock variant. The two stock types required different receivers that were not interchangeable. The common usage (Western) designations have been included in parentheses.

Weapon Production and Use

The following nations are believed to have manufactured 7.62×39mm AK type rifles: Albania, Bangladesh, Bulgaria, Cambodia, People's Republic of China, Cuba, Egypt, Ethiopia, German Democratic Republic (East Germany), Hungary, India, Iran, Iraq, Democratic People's Republic of Korea (North Korea), Nigeria, Pakistan, Poland, Romania, Serbia, Slovenia, Sudan, Vietnam, Venezuela and Yugoslavia.

The following list, although not considered exhaustive, lists known users of the 7.62mm AK rifles, with the weapons being a primary armament or specialist issue; Afghanistan, Albania, Algeria, Angola, Armenia, Azerbaijan, Bangladesh, Benin, Bhutan, Bosnia and Herzegovina, Botswana, Bulgaria, Cambodia, Cameroon, Cape Verde, Central

Egyptian memorial on the east bank of the Suez Canal, near Ismailia, commemorating the soldiers who lost their lives in the 1973 conflict with Israel. The memorial is a stylized AK bayonet some 66m (200ft) in height. *Gunnery Sgt Keith A. Milks USMC*

African Republic, Chad, Chile, People's Republic of China, Comoros, Congo-Brazzaville, Democratic Republic of Congo, Croatia, Cuba, Egypt, Eritrea, Ethiopia, Equatorial Guinea, Ethiopia, Gabon, Georgia, German Democratic Republic (East Germany), Greece, Guinea-Bissau, Guyana, Honduras, Hungary, India, Indonesia, Iran, Iraq, Israel, Kenya, Democratic People's Republic of Korea (North Korea), Kosovo, Laos, Lebanon, Lesotho, Liberia, Libya, Macedonia, Madagascar, Mali, Malta, Morocco, Mongolia, Montenegro, Mozambique, Namibia, Nicaragua, Nigeria, Pakistan, Palestine, Peru, Philippines, Poland, Qatar, Romania, Russia, Rwanda, São Tomé and Principe, Sahrawi Arab Democratic Republic, Serbia, Seychelles, Sierra Leone, Slovenia, Somalia, Soviet Union, Sri Lanka, Sudan, Surinam, Syria, Tanzania, Togo, Turkey, Ukraine, United Arab Emirates, Vietnam, Yemen, Yugoslavia, Zaire, Zambia and Zimbabwe.

Albania (Republic of)

Albania began work on a weapon production facility in the town of Gramsh in 1962. Prior to this the country had relied wholly on imports, mainly from the Soviet Union, with whom they had been allied until 1960 when they broke off relations. The first weapons to be made in Albania were manufactured in 1966 and were copies of the Chinese Type 56 carbine (itself a copy of the Soviet SKS rifle). In 1974 the Albanian state arsenal Um Gramsh received a licence from China North Industries Corporation (Norinco) to produce a Kalashnikov type assault rifle. The Albanian assault rifle was accepted into service as the Automatiku Shqiptar 78 (ASh78). It was a direct copy of the Chinese Type 56 rifle with stamped receiver, the pattern having no magazine guide depressions. Albania used imported weapons and made up weapons using imported components. Albania also produced a grenade-launching version of the ASh78. Only made in small numbers, the weapon had a removable tubular grenade launcher and had the rear sight repositioned on the front hinged receiver cover. A small lever on the right side of the gas block cut off the flow of gas to the piston when launching grenades.

The ASh78 differs only in minor detail from the Chinese Type 56. There is no receiver marking for safe, but full automatic is marked by an 'A' and single shot by a '1'. The markings are stamped by hand and are occasionally illegible or hardly discernible.

Calibre 7.62×39mm ammo for the ASh78 was produced at the Polican Arsenal, the country's main ammunition works.

Albanian sources claim that as many as 26,000 rifles of various patterns were produced annually. By the mid-1990s, however, the management of state concerns had deteriorated to such a degree that little military equipment was being produced. In 2004 the UN Department for Disarmament Affairs stated that there was no longer any effective state-run military production facility in Albania. Indeed, under UN disarmament control 141,000 Albanian small arms were destroyed between 1997 and 2004. However, there were extensive stockpiles of weaponry and ammunition and in 2002 Albania exported 600 ASh78 rifles to Afghanistan. A further 30,000 ASh78s were sent to Afghanistan in late 2010. Some 200 ASh78 rifles were also exported to Germany in 2004, apparently destined for the international collectors market. At the time of writing it is believed that small arms production in Albania has effectively ceased.

Albanian-made variant of the Chinese Type 56 stamped receiver rifle, the ASh78 Type 1 (Automatiku Shqiptar 78 Tip-1). This weapon differs only in minor detail from the Chinese original, most noticeably the sight block, the receiver markings and the flat-sided receiver with no magazine guide depression. (Although not common this feature can also be found on some Chinese-made Type 56 rifles and Iraqi Tabuks.) Media Image Photography

Left side of the Albanian ASh78 rifle. Although lacking any manufacturers' markings, these weapons were made at the Gramsh state arsenal, located at Um Gramsh. Media Image Photography

Detail of the left side receiver showing the individually hand-stamped numerals of the serial number followed by 84, indicating manufacture in 1984. Media Image Photography

ASh78 Type 1 selector lever set at automatic. The automatic position of the ASh78 was marked with an 'A' (here concealed by the selector lever) and a '1' for single shot. The single shot position '1' of this weapon is somewhat poorly stamped. Media Image Photography

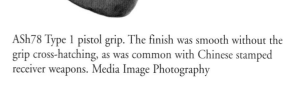

ASh78 Type 1 pistol grip. The finish was smooth without the grip cross-hatching, as was common with Chinese stamped receiver weapons. Media Image Photography

Albanian soldier armed with an AKS type rifle during Operation *Cooperative Osprey*, held at Camp Lejeune, North Carolina, during 1996. The style of the weapon's foresight block suggests a Chinese pattern milled receiver Type 56-1 rifle, but the folding stock is distinctly of the Russian type rather than Chinese. Albanian weapons are usually fitted with Chinese pattern slings. US Department of Defense

Detail of the ASh78 Type 1 sight graduated to 800m (2,600ft) and with a battle sight marking shown as a 'D'. Media Image Photography

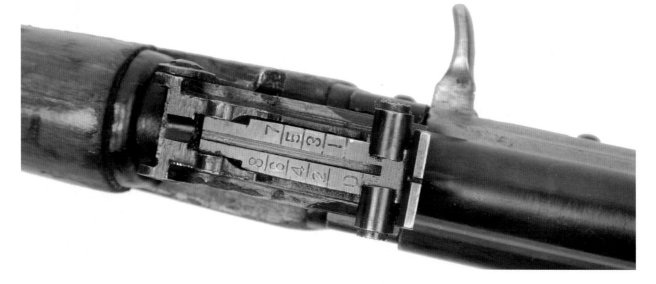

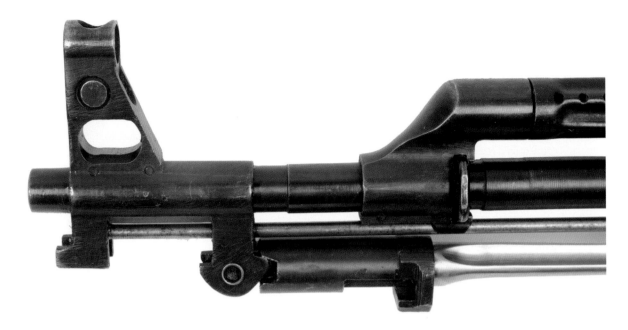

Foresight block and bayonet mechanism of the ASh78 Type 1. The sight block is uniquely Albanian, a hybrid of the Chinese and Russian patterns. Media Image Photography

Rather weary ASh78 Type 1 rifles found alongside other ordnance concealed in flour sacks. The cache was discovered by US troops undertaking search operations near the Kosovan town of Goden during August 2001. US Department of Defense

Bulgaria

The original AK weapons used by Bulgaria were imported from Poland and Russia. By the early 1960s weapons were being constructed using imported components with domestic production starting soon after at the Kazanlak arsenal in central Bulgaria. The AKK was a copy of the Russian type 3 milled receiver AK with the AKKS being the Bulgarian version of the folding stock AKS. While imported weapons bear Polish or Russian manufacturers' markings, Bulgarian-made weapons are marked with a '10' within a double circle. Weapons made in Bulgaria from imported components can be found to bear both the original factory markings and Bulgarian marks.

Bulgaria also undertook local production of the stamped receiver AKM, with the Bulgarian variants being the fixed stock AKKM and the folding stock AKKMS, but the AKK and AKKS patterns remained predominant in Bulgarian service.

Following the fall of Communism Bulgaria made efforts at exporting AK weapons of various patterns. Importantly, the plant at Kazanlak, now called Arsenal JSCo, capitalized on the worldwide availability of 7.62×39mm ammunition and by 2000 was offering no fewer than eight modern variants of the type 3 milled receiver AKK and AKKS rifles, designated the AR series. The primary variants were the fixed stock AR and the ARF with under-folding stock. The guns had black polyamide plastic furniture and AK74 type flash hiders or, less commonly, plain AK type muzzle nuts. Shortly after the overthrow of Saddam Hussein the Iraqi National Guard undertook a contract with Bulgaria for the supply of AR rifles. Typically many of the weapons supplied under the contract found their way into the hands of insurgents.

Bulgaria also produced its own AK47 and AKM type bayonets. The AKM I and AKM II bayonets were standard on the AKK and AKKS rifles, but the AR and ARF series were fitted with the AK74 type bayonet with its distinctive grip style (sometimes called the AKM III bayonet).

Like those from Romania and Hungary, Bulgarian weapons were issued with a leather sling. The Bulgarian sling was quite distinct and complicated in its design. Its construction used no fewer than seven sections of leather and required separate end tabs secured by plastic studs. By comparison the Romanian sling used only two sections of leather. The leather slings were eventually replaced by a Soviet style webbing sling.

Standard Variants

AKK	Type 3A receiver, fixed stock
AKKS	Type 3B receiver, under-folding stock
AKKM	Type 4A receiver, fixed stock
AKKMS	Type 4B receiver, under-folding stock
AR	New production milled Type 3A receiver, fixed stock
ARF	New production milled Type 3B receiver, under-folding stock

Photographed in 1961, a Bulgarian army Junior Sergeant poses proudly with his AKK rifle. Private collection

Soviet-made AKK (AK) rifle fitted with Bulgarian red polyamide plastic stock, pistol grip and handguards. Prior to Bulgarian domestic production, many complete weapons, bayonets and individual components were supplied to Bulgaria by both the Soviet Union and Poland. This weapon bears Russian selector markings and the Izhmash 'arrow in triangle' logo. Media Image Photography

Receiver markings of the AKK (AK) rifle showing the 'arrow in triangle' marking of the Izhmash engineering plant, located in Izhevsk, and the weapon's serial number. This view clearly shows the large milled-out section above the magazine housing of the type 3 receiver. Unlike the type 2 receiver milling, which was parallel with the barrel axis, that of the type 3 is parallel to the sloped bottom edge of the receiver. Media Image Photography

Milled receiver Bulgarian AKK rifle. Identical to the Soviet AK, the Bulgarian weapon has Bulgarian Cyrillic selector markings and the 'double circle 10' marking of the state military factory at Kazanlak. It was made in 1971. Many weapons made up from imported components often bear both the markings of the originating factory (such as a Russian Izhmash arrow or a Polish 'oval 11') and the Bulgarian assembling plant's 'double circle 10'. Media Image Photography

Receiver markings of the AKK rifle, showing the 'double circle 10' marking of the state military factory at Kazanlak, the date 1971 and the weapon's serial number. Media Image Photography

Bulgarian AKK Cyrillic selector markings, with the selector set at Avomat (full automatic). The single shot setting is marked with a Cyrillic 'ED' for Endo. Media Image Photography

Bulgarian AKK rear sight ranged from 100 to 800m. The 350m battle sight position is marked with a Cyrillic 'P'. Media Image Photography

Sight block and barrel of the AKK. The original barrel muzzle nut found on milled receiver AKs has been replaced by a muzzle brake, a simple way of upgrading the performance of the AK by reducing the weapon's tendency to kick upward and to the right. Media Image Photography

Detail of the pistol grip of the Bulgarian AKK. The plastic stud used to fasten Bulgarian slings is evident in this image. Media Image Photography

Milled receiver folding stock Soviet AKS rifle with Bulgarian red plastic handguards, called the AKKS in Bulgarian service. This weapon has the early slab-sided magazine. Domestic production of AK rifles began in Bulgaria in 1967. Media Image Photography

Left side of the Soviet-made AKKS with folding stock in the closed position. The weapon was made at the Izhmash factory. Media Image Photography

Soviet-made AKKS rifle (AKS) folding stock. The stamped steel stock used with Soviet AKS rifles was of quite a sturdy construction. Media Image Photography

An Afghan National Army (ANA) soldier armed with a well-worn AKK rifle, retaining its original Bulgarian leather sling, during a joint ANA/USMC operation in 2009. The weapon has been given a make-over with the addition of blue tape over the woodwork and magazine. Whilet it has long been a common practice to use white tape on weapons during operations in snowy environments, the blue tape has considerably less camouflage value but improved 'street cred'. US Department of Defense

A Bulgarian sailor armed with an AKK rifle and fixed bayonet, photographed during the visit of the dock landing ship USS Whidbey Island to the Bulgarian port of Burgas, 1992. US Department of Defense

A Bulgarian soldier, armed with a pristine example of an AKKS rifle, photographed during joint US/Bulgarian training held at Camp Lejeune, North Carolina, during 1996. US Department of Defense

Bulgarian Special Forces soldiers on Exercise Cooperative Key, held in Bulgaria during 2003. The soldier carries the AKKMS, the Bulgarian version of the AKMS. He wears a splinter pattern assault vest with integral magazine pouches. US Department of Defense

Bulgarian AR rifle, a twenty-first-century production of the milled receiver AKK. The weapon has a dull black finish with AK74 type black plastic furniture and grey phosphate-coated rear sight and bolt carrier. This particular weapon uses the AK74 style gas block but the standard AK type was also used. The AR rifle is also available with an AK74 type flash eliminator. Media Image Photography

The AR rifle's serial number KO 36 5443 is engraved above the milled section of the receiver. The last four figures are repeated on the receiver cover. Also shown is the 'double circle 10' marking of the state military factory at Kazanlak. Media Image Photography

Detail of the forward left side of the AR rifle showing the AK74 style gas block and black plastic fore-end and handguard. Media Image Photography

Bulgarian AR rifle's rear sight ranged from 100 to 800m. The grey phosphate finish sight is set at 100m. Media Image Photography

An Iraqi soldier photographed in Baghdad during 2007. He is armed with a Bulgarian AR rifle with standard AK gas block. These weapons were imported into Iraq in 2004 for use by the Iraqi National Guard, then under US command. (By November of the same year a number of AR rifles had already reached the hands of insurgents in Fallujah.) This was at a time of severe weapon shortages for re-armament. Domestic production had ceased and coalition forces had destroyed most of the Iraqi weapons they found. The National Guard was absorbed into the Army in January 2005. US Department of Defense

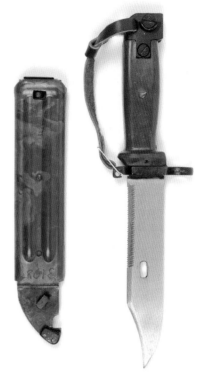

Bulgarian sling types: (top) AKK rifle fitted with the standard pattern leather sling threaded through a wire loop fitting on the rear left receiver with the front attached by a spring clip to the gas block sling loop; (centre) leather sling showing leather end tabs with plastic studs and double buckle arrangement; (bottom) late production green webbing sling. Media Image Photography

Bulgarian-manufacture AKM II bayonet for the AKKM and AKKMS rifles. A close copy of the Russian bayonet, the grips and scabbard are a mottled orange plastic. Media Image Photography

Bulgarian splinter pattern camouflage cover for the AKKS rifle. This lightweight fabric cover has a separate muzzle cover and openings for the sights, cocking lever and trigger, suggesting that it was designed to allow the weapon to be used in an emergency without removing the cover. Media Image Photography

Typical Bulgarian four-pocket magazine pouch. Media Image Photography

Bulgarian-manufacture AKM II bayonet showing grip detail with impressed 'double circle 10' logo. Media Image Photography

Bulgarian combination tool (left to right): combination tool (the cap forms the rod guide for cleaning the bore and the tool itself is used to store the other implements), jag, bore brush and screwdriver/drift that also serves as a foresight adjustment tool. The complete combination tool is stored inside the magazine pouch. At right is the oil bottle that was stored in the magazine pouch's small external pocket. Media Image Photography

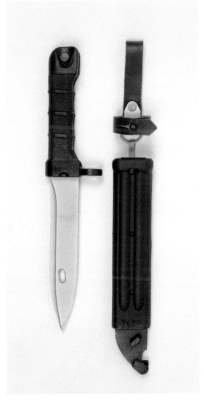

The Warsaw Pact nations were well versed in the art of warfare in nuclear, biological and chemically contaminated environments. This Bulgarian-issue plastic bottle contained decontamination fluid for use on personal weapons that had been exposed to such contaminants. The top incorporated plastic bristles to assist in scrubbing the weapons, which, unlike the troops who wore rubber suits and gas masks, could not easily be protected. The leather sling would need to be discarded as it could not be decontaminated. Media Image Photography

Bulgarian AK74 bayonet. Although this bayonet is standard for the AK74, it was also issued with the Bulgarian AR series of rifles, marrying the early type 3 milled receiver Kalashnikov with the latest pattern of bayonet. Media Image Photography

Bulgarian-manufacture AK bayonets for the AKK and AKKS rifles showing minor differences in manufacturing: (left) bayonet scabbard with green vinyl hanger; (centre) bayonet scabbard with all-leather hanger; (right) scabbard with green webbing hanger and leather strap. The bayonet shows the left side with a typical Bulgarian style serial number on the pommel. Media Image Photography

China (People's Republic of)

The People's Republic of China adopted the type 3 milled receiver AK in 1956. They were direct copies of the Soviet weapon with fixed (Type 56 Rifle) or folding (Type 56-1 Rifle) stock and allowed fitting of the standard AK47 bayonet. A fixed stock Type 56 rifle with a distinct triangular-bladed folding bayonet was soon introduced, a pattern that was to become synonymous with the Chinese weapons and one of the most recognizable AK types. The Chinese eventually switched to producing a variant of the AKMS that, surprisingly, retained the same designations of the original milled weapons, Type 56 and Type 56-1. Unlike the Soviet AKMS, the Chinese stamped receiver Type 56 retained the plain type receiver cover, white metal bolt carrier, large foresight post and 800m (2,600ft) sights of the AK type weapons. Both the milled receiver and stamped receiver Type 56 can be found with a barrel nut or a plain barrel end. None of the Type 56 rifle types intended for military use were fitted with a muzzle brake. Interestingly, the Chinese version of the SKS rifle was also designated the Type 56 but classed as a carbine rather than a rifle like the AK type weapons.

The classic under-folding stock of the Type 56-1 rifle was upgraded with the introduction of the Type 56-2 rifle with side-folding stock. The stock had an inset plastic cheek rest that doubled as a handgrip. The side-folding stock of the Type 56-2 allowed it to be built on the standard Type 56 (fixed stock) receiver.

The Chinese built up a major export market for their Type 56 rifles, many thousands seeing use in Vietnam and other major and minor conflicts worldwide, and later being used in Iraq and Afghanistan. Indigenous weapons were marked with Chinese selector markings with export weapons being marked with an 'L' (Automatic) and 'D' (single shot) settings. The weapons were also very popular with American sports shooters and many civilian variants of the military rifles were imported into the USA. China North Industries Corporation (Norinco) provided the export hub for Chinese weapons.

The Chinese made a copy of the Soviet AK47 bayonet with wood grips, although the most recognizable Chinese bayonet is the triangular folding type. An AK47 bayonet with wood grips was also produced solely for export to the USA; it is clearly marked 'MADE IN CHINA'. A bayonet based on the AKM II was also produced with a plain blade and no wire-cutter, but it is believed that this also was only made for export for the American collector and shooting market. While the plain bladed bayonet is quite common, a rare variant comprising a standard AKM II with the wire-cutter blade and scabbard fittings is known to have been produced in limited numbers, again possibly only for export.

Chinese slings were usually of webbing although a leather sling was made in fewer numbers. Direct copies of the Soviet pattern sling are uncommon. The standard type is made up of a section of webbing with buckle adjustment metal D rings at each end with leather tabs. This type was further simplified by deleting the rear D ring and tab and feeding the web sling straight through the rear sling swivel.

Standard Variants

Type 56	Type 3A receiver, fixed stock
Type 56	Type 3A receiver, fixed stock. Integral folding spike bayonet
Type 56-1	Type 3B receiver, under-folding stock
Type 56-1	Type 3B receiver, under-folding stock. Integral folding spike bayonet
Type 56	Type 4A receiver, fixed stock. Integral folding spike bayonet
Type 56-1	Type 4B receiver, under-folding stock
Type 56-1	Type 4B receiver, under-folding stock. Integral folding spike bayonet
Type 56-2	Type 4A receiver, side-folding stock

Chinese Type 56 rifle. Based on the third pattern milled receiver AK, it differs in minor detail, most noticeably the foresight, which is fully enclosed rather than having 'ears'. Many of these weapons were exported to the North Vietnamese Army and Viet Cong during the Vietnam War (1955–75). Media Image Photography

Detail of the right side of the receiver showing the 'L' (Automatic) and 'D' (single shot) selector markings associated with export variants of the Type 56. Media Image Photography

Type 56 milled receiver left side showing the manufacturer's factory marking of a '66' within a triangle and the Chinese characters for Type 56, followed by the weapon serial number. Media Image Photography

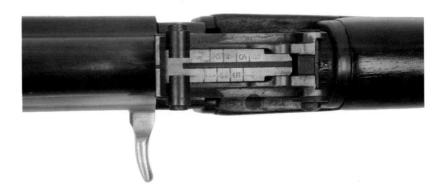

Rear sight of the milled receiver Type 56 rifle showing graduations to 800m and the 'D' mark indicating the battle sight position. Media Image Photography

Wood pistol grip of the milled receiver Type 56 rifle. The grip is a direct copy of that used on the Russian AK rifle. Media Image Photography

A communist soldier stands beneath the Viet Cong flag during an exchange of POWs held at Loc Ninh by the Four Power Joint Military Commission during 1973. He carries a milled receiver Chinese Type 56 rifle. US Department of Defense

North Vietnamese workers parade with Chinese Type 56 milled receiver rifles. These weapons are the variant fitted with a permanently attached folding spike bayonet. Private collection

A Special Forces LRRP (Long Range Reconnaissance Patrol) GI of the First Cavalry Division operating in Vietnam during 1969. The soldier carries a captured Chinese third pattern milled receiver Type 56 rifle with folding stock and Chinese pattern sling with leather end tabs. Terry Moon (First Cavalry Division, Vietnam, 1969)

Chinese Type 56 rifle. Based on the Russian AKM, it has a permanently attached folding bayonet. When the Chinese changed from the milled receiver (AK type) to the stamped pattern (AKM type) there was no change in the standard rifle designation. Media Image Photography

Detail of the front of the Chinese Type 56 rifle with the triangular spike bayonet in the folded position below the barrel. The chisel tip of the bayonet is fitted into a groove beneath the wooden fore-end, preventing unnecessary injury. Media Image Photography

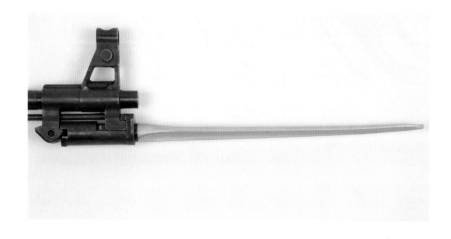

Detail of the barrel and foresight post of the Chinese Type 56 rifle with the triangular spike bayonet in the extended position. Media Image Photography

Right side of the receiver of the Type 56 rifle showing the selector lever and markings 'L' for automatic and 'D' for single shot. Media Image Photography

Detail of the stamped receiver Type 56 rifle, left side, showing the trunnion markings. This weapon was made at state factory 962. The weapon retained the plain receiver cover used with the earlier machined receiver Type 56 rifle. Media Image Photography

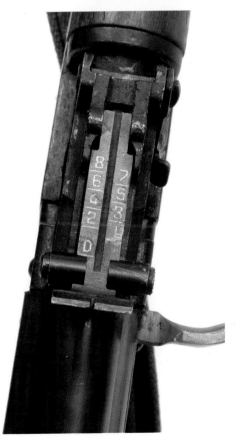

Rear sight of the stamped receiver Type 56 rifle showing graduations to 800m, unlike the standard AKM rifle sights that were graduated to 1,000m. Media Image Photography

Wooden pistol grip of the Type 56 rifle with stamped receiver. Media Image Photography

Foresight of the stamped receiver Type 56 rifle showing the bayonet mechanism in folded position. Media Image Photography

A Beninese soldier photographed using a pull-through to clean the barrel of his Chinese stamped receiver Type 56 rifle, Benin, 2009. US Department of Defense

Qingdao, China, 1986. A Chinese sailor parades with a stamped receiver Type 56 rifle. The rifle is the variant that has a plain receiver with no dimple above the magazine housing (the pattern also produced by Albania). US Department of Defense

Chinese Type 56-1 rifle with stamped receiver and under-folding stock. The receiver was not interchangeable with that of the Type 56 rifle. Media Image Photography

Chinese Type 56-1 rifle, left side, showing the folding stock in the closed position. The Type 56-1 can also be found with a folding bayonet. Media Image Photography

Detail of the selector lever markings on the Type 56-1 rifle, showing the type 1 selector lever in the safe position and the Chinese markings. Media Image Photography

Left side of a Type 56-1 rifle showing the designation markings on the trunnion: the state factory mark of a '66' within a triangle, the designation 56-1 and the serial number. Media Image Photography

Type 56-1 sight block, barrel and gas tube assembly (also used on the Type 56-2). The rifle muzzle is plain and unthreaded with no provision for a muzzle brake or grenade launcher. The Chinese retained the gas tube vents, as used on the AK type weapons, on their Type 56 stamped receiver rifles. AKM variants usually have the vents integral to the gas block. This Type 56-1 has no provision for a bayonet. Media Image Photograph

Type 56-1 pistol grip and detail of the right side of the folding stock pivot. Media Image Photography

Type 56-1 folding stock in the open position. Also shown are the stock release catch and integral rear sling swivel. Media Image Photography

Type 56-2 rifle. This weapon was not an improved Type 56-1 but was actually based on the Type 56 rifle, though with a side-folding stock and plastic furniture. It used the same receiver as the Type 56 rifle and retains the plain receiver cover, but has the second pattern selector lever with central reinforced rib. Media Image Photography

Type 56-2 rifle with the stock folded along the right side of the receiver. When folded the stock hindered use of the selector lever. The Type 56-2 uses the same sight block as the Type 56-1 rifle. This example has no provision for the attachment of a bayonet but a variant of the Type 56-2 has fittings for an AKM style bayonet. Media Image Photography

Left side of the Type 56-2 rifle's receiver showing the designation markings on the trunnion: the state factory mark of a '66' within a triangle, the designation 56-2 and the serial number. Media Image Photography

Type 56-2 pistol grip and detail of the right side of the folding stock release catch and hinge. Although not common, this type of grip can occasionally be found on Type 56 and Type 56-1 rifles. Media Image Photography

At first glance this weapon appears to be a Type 56-2 rifle fitted with an East German folding stock. It is in fact a modified standard Type 56 rifle. The Type 56 wooden stock has been removed and a hand-crafted folding stock has been crudely fitted. While resembling the East German style folding stock, it is quite basic in construction and differs in some detail. Additionally, the folding bayonet has been removed and the mechanism has been cut away from the foresight post. This weapon was used in the Balkan conflict and was undoubtedly modified in theatre. It is fitted with a Yugoslav magazine. Media Image Photography

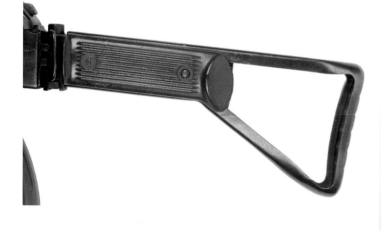

Detail of the Type 56-2 rifle's folding stock showing the plastic cheek piece set into the stock. This also served as a grip during bayonet fighting (where a fitting for a bayonet was provided) and hand-to-hand combat. Media Image Photography

The side-folding stock Type 56 rifle with the stock closed against the receiver. Media Image Photography

A Bangladeshi naval rating fires a Type 56-2 assault rifle onboard the BNS Bangabandhu during an exercise held in September 2011. The photographer has caught the weapon's action in the fully rearward position, with an ejected cartridge case visible just above the handguard. The selector lever is clearly set to single shot. US Department of Defense

Side-folding Type 56 rifle receiver showing the trunnion markings. These consist of the state factory marking of 5506, the designation (Type) 56 and the weapon serial number, showing the weapon's true origin as a Type 56 and not a Type 56-2. Media Image Photography

Detail of the foresight post and barrel of the side-folding Type 56, showing the narrow section of barrel immediately behind the sight post. This is where the bayonet mounting mechanism would have been fitted. The top of the sight post has also been ground to resemble the standard open top sight. The end of the barrel is plain and not fitted with a barrel nut; despite the appearance, it is not threaded. Media Image Photography

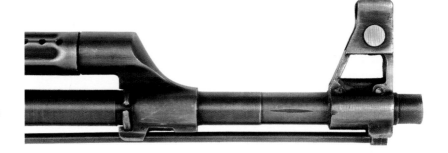

The Type 56-2 style pistol grip fitted to the Type 56 rifle with side-folding stock. The rather rough finish of the hand-made folding stock hinge and arm is also evident in this image. Media Image Photography

Chinese five-pocket magazine pouch. The pouch has a web shoulder strap, two belt loops at the rear and external pockets for the combination tool and oil container. As with most Chinese equipment, the pocket flaps and top flap are closed with wooden toggles. This pouch was made in 1970 by state factory number 3521. At right are two Chinese-made magazines, which lack the rear rib of other nationalities' productions and have two full-width horizontal ribs at the lower edge. At left is a standard magazine and at right a stamped pattern with integral side plate impressed into the upper part of the magazine. Media Image Photography

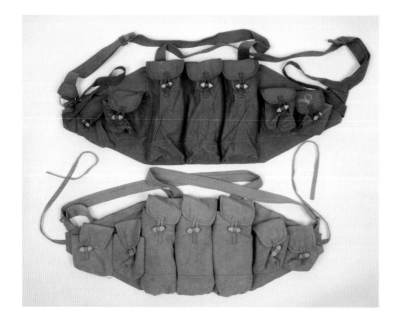

Chinese-manufacture chest pouch for three 30-round magazines. The rear of the pouch is stamped with Chinese characters including 'Type 56-1' and '7.62mm'. Below is a copy of the Chinese pouch issued to North Vietnam Army troops during the Vietnam War and believed to have been made there. This style of magazine carrier has seen use with many nations and is popular with insurgent forces. Media Image Photography

Stock hinge mechanism of the Type 56 rifle with side-folding stock. As with the East German folding stock on which this example was modelled, it uses the tang (normally used to fit the wooden stock) to attach the folding stock. However, it lacks the high-quality finish of the East German original. Media Image Photography

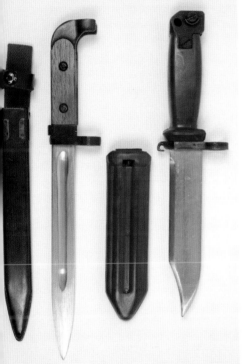

Chinese knife bayonets. At left is the standard AK type bayonet and at right an AKM II hybrid without the serrated blade and with no provision for it to be used as a wire-cutter. This pattern, an export model not used by the Chinese, was also manufactured with black scabbard and grips. Media Image Photography

Stock hinge mechanism of the Type 56 rifle with side-folding stock. As with the East German folding stock, that this example was modelled on, it also uses the tang (normally used to fit the wooden stock) to attach the folding stock. However, it lacks the high quality finish of the East German original. Media Image Photography

Typical Chinese sling patterns. The sling fitted to the Chinese Type 56 rifle is a copy of the standard Russian AK sling. Below is an economy variant that required less metalwork, using D rings with leather tabs. Bottom is a pattern that has a single D ring and leather tab, reducing costs to a minimum. Media Image Photography

Egypt

In 1955 Egypt forged ties with the Warsaw Pact, obtaining military aid from the Soviet Union, Czechoslovakia and later East Germany. This was to include Soviet and East German Kalashnikov rifles. Domestic production of the AKM was eventually licensed to the Maadi arms factory, with the new rifle being designated the Misr (being the ancient Arabic name for Egypt). The folding stock version used a side folder based on the standard East German pattern but using a crutch-style butt plate. This style of stock had been provided on MPiKMS export rifles imported from East Germany and the fixed and folding stock versions of the Maadi used the same receiver as on the German MPiKM and MPiKMS. The design of the folding stock also allowed easy use of the selector lever when the stock was folded. Images of Egyptian troops show that an AKMS with under-folding stock is also used, but the nation of manufacture has not been determined.

Egypt was eventually to become a major arms exporter in its own right. During the 1980s large numbers of Misr rifles were exported worldwide. While weaponry intended for domestica use had Arabic script selector markings, those manufactured for export used the Latin (Roman) script markings 'S' for safe, 'A' for automatic and 'R' for repetition/single shot. Sight ranges on domestic weapons were marked in Eastern Arabic numerals, while export weapons were marked with standard Arabic numerals.

The Egyptians have also made the AKM II type bayonet. Early production was of the 'transitional' style using the AKM I type scabbard with rubber grip section, matched with an AKM II bayonet with black or brown grips. The quality of production was very poor when compared to bayonets of European manufacture. Later production Maadi bayonets were of the standard AKM II type with orange plastic scabbard and grips; these were usually marked with the Maadi factory logo and were of an improved quality.

Egyptian slings are generally of a green, loose-weave cotton with very low quality, thin-gauge metal fittings and leatherette tension sliders.

The Standard Misr assault rifle with wooden furniture, manufactured by the arms factory Maadi. It is a stamped receiver AKM pattern weapon. Media Image Photography

Barrel, cleaning rod, muzzle brake and foresight post of the Misr rifle. The sight block is the standard AKM style.
Media Image Photography

Right side of the Misr receiver showing the selector lever, set in the automatic fire position and the Arabic selector markings. Note also that the bolt carrier has a black finish. Media Image Photography

Left side of the Misr receiver showing Arabic markings (including the calibre 7.62×39) on the sight block, and the serial number on the trunnion. The serial number is preceded by the year 1988 (in Eastern Arabic numerals) and the Maadi factory logo. This image clearly shows the black painted finish common to all Egyptian AKs. Media Image Photography

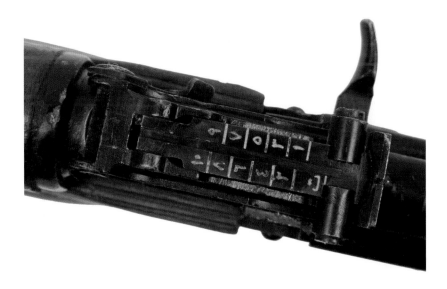

Misr rear sight showing ten range graduations and the battle sight position marked in Arabic. The sight position shown is set to battle sight, equating to 350m. Media Image Photography

Misr rifle with the unique Egyptian pattern of side-folding stock. The receiver group is the same as that used on the standard rifle and the folding stock fits to the rear of the receiver in place of the wood stock (unlike Russian receivers, where those for the AKMS and the AKM are not interchangeable). This design principle was copied from the East German MPiKMS but differs in the detail. Media Image Photography

Misr rifle with side-folding stock in the closed position against the right side of the receiver. The folded stock does not interfere with weapon function or selector lever. This Misr is an export version with the selector markings reading 'S A R' (Safe, Automatic and Repetition/single shot) rather than showing Arabic script. Media Image Photography

Detail of the rear of the receiver of the Misr folding stock rifle showing the stock's hinge block, release catch and rear sling swivel. Media Image Photography

The Misr rifle's folding stock showing the unique 'crutch' style butt and straight stock. Media Image Photography

Detail of the left side of the Misr folding-stock rifle showing the markings, the calibre marking on the sight block and serial number on the trunnion. The sight block is marked 'CAL. 7.62×39 mm' on this export weapon. Media Image Photography

Detail of the rear sight on the Misr folding-stock rifle showing the range markings used on the export weapon, with a 'P' signifying the battle sight position. Media Image Photography

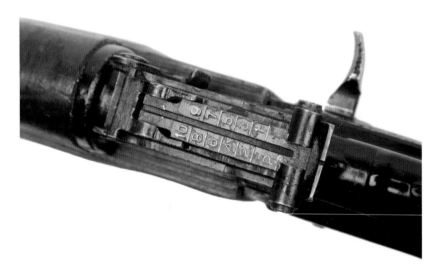

The black plastic grip used on the Misr folding-stock export rifle. Grips were also made in brown and brick red. Media Image Photography

Egyptian Misr rifle selector lever showing the markings used on export weapons. The selector positions are 'S A R'. Media Image Photography

Early pattern Egyptian AKM Type II bayonets used with the Misr assault rifle. The poor quality is evident in this picture with obvious gaps between the grips and the crossguard and pommel being filled with resin. Early bayonets used the AKM I type scabbard, but later productions had orange grips and the standard orange plastic AKM II type scabbard. Media Image Photography

An Egyptian tourist policeman on duty at the Pyramids in Cairo. He is armed with a well-used Misr rifle. Toby Brayley

Bayonet fixed, an Egyptian Marine takes aim with his Misr rifle during an amphibious assault held as a part of Exercise Bright Star 85. The AK stands up well to use in such sandy terrain. US Department of Defense

Egyptian webbing slings used with the Misr assault rifle. The poor quality sling is threaded through the sling loop on the lower rear edge of the wooden stock and attached to the gas block swivel using the spring clip. Below is a well-used Egyptian sling of particularly poor construction. The buckle is lightweight stamped metal with unfinished edges and the D ring and spring clip are made from a narrow gauge wire. Media Image Photography

An Iraqi Tactical Support Unit (SWAT) officer armed with an Egyptian export variant of the Misr rifle photographed during operations in Basra, Iraq, during 2005. Author's photograph

East Germany (German Democratic Republic)

Soviet-occupied East Germany remained without an army until 1956, in which year the Nationale Volksarmee (NVA) was formed. Like most eastern European nations falling under Soviet control, the NVA was initially armed with old Russian weapons, principally the PPSh 41 and the Mosin Nagant M1944 carbine. In 1957 a licence was granted to build a copy of the type 3 milled receiver AK. The first MPiK (Maschinenpistole Kalaschnikow) was produced in 1958 with full production commencing soon after. An under-folding stock variant was issued as the MPiKS (Maschinenpistole Kalaschnikow mit Schulterstütze).

The Soviet stamped receiver AKMS was put in production in East Germany during 1967. The MPiKM (Maschinenpistole Kalaschnikow Modernisier) was initially made with a wood stock, fore-end and handguard. These components were progressively replaced by brown plastic ones and weapons can be found with a mixture of wood and plastic furniture. In 1972 the East Germans introduced the MPiKMS (Maschinenpistole Kalaschnikow Modernisier mit Schulterstütze) with its distinctive side-folding stock, built on a standard MPiKM stamped receiver. It is sometimes referred to as the MPiKMS 72. East Germany had a thriving export market in MPiK type weapons and the unique stock used on the MPiKMS was copied in principle by a number of foreign manufacturers as it reduced production costs by permitting the use of a standard receiver type on both fixed and folding stock weapons. It also allowed unhindered access to the selector lever, unlike the Soviet pattern under-folding stock. East German selector markings were 'E' (Einzelfeuer) for single shot and 'D' (Dauerfeuer) for full automatic. The safe position was unmarked.

East Germany produced versions of the AK47, AKM I and AKM II bayonets for use with the MPiK/MPiKM series of weapons. They usually have distinctive black plastic grips but a rare variant has red grips. The Seitengewehr 47 (AK47) bayonets have grey webbing hangers to the scabbard, while the Seitengewehr 59 (AKM I) and Seitengewehr AK74 (AKM II) have grey leather hangers. The bayonets are otherwise similar to the Soviet originals. The Seitengewehr AK74 was not produced for use with 7.62mm weapons but rather for the 5.45×39mm MPiAK74, although the Seitengewehr 59 and Seitengewehr AK74 were interchangeable with either rifle.

The NVA used a stylized wooden training rifle and bayonet. The rifle had a wood stock and magazine with a metal barrel in the simplified form of an MPiK. The end of the barrel could be fitted with a simple tubular training bayonet formed from a spring-loaded, rubber-tipped plunger and a metal body with rubber grip allowing the bayonet to be used as a hand-held knife when not fitted to the training rifle. The training rifle had its own distinct pattern of lightweight grey webbing sling.

Load-bearing field equipment used by the NVA was of grey webbing. To match this, the slings used with their rifles were also made of grey webbing. The early MPiK and MPiKS used a grey web version of the standard Soviet sling. The later stamped receiver MPiKM and MPiKMS types had narrow sling swivels that would not accept the Soviet-style sling. These weapons used a distinctive narrow gauge nylon webbing sling with double buckle, plastic keepers and without the D ring and carbine hook. It would probably have been impossible to make a cheaper sling without entirely prejudicing its functionality.

Standard Variants

MPiK	Type 3A receiver, fixed stock
MPiKS	Type 3B receiver, under-folding stock
MPiKM	Type 4A receiver, fixed stock
MPiKMS (72)	Type 4A receiver, side-folding stock

East German MPiKM rifle. Based on the Soviet AKM, this MPiKM has a plastic handguard to the gas tube with a wooden fore-end, plastic pistol grip and dimpled plastic stock. The stock has no provision for a combination tool, which is carried in the soldier's field equipment; unlike the MPiK, however, the MPiKM is issued with a cleaning rod. Media Image Photography

East German MPiK in use with Nationale Volksarmee conscripts under training. The MPiK was not issued with the cleaning rod as NVA conscripts were required to use a pull-through to clean the weapon bore. This weapon is fitted with a blank firing adaptor (BFA) and Zusatzvisier zum Nachtschiessen 64 (ZVN-64, additional sights for night firing). Private collection

The folding-stock MPiKS in use with an NVA mortar team during the early 1960s. The men wear the Flächentarn camouflage uniform. Private collection

Detail of the MPiKM rifle selector lever. The selector is set to 'E' (Einzelfeuer) for single shot, the 'D' being Dauerfeuer for fully automatic. The selector rests against the selector stop, which is part of the magazine release catch housing. It prevents the lever being forced down too far and is common to all AKM type weapons. Media Image Photography

Rear sight block, trunnion and front of the MPiKM receiver. Typical of many post-unification weapons, the original serial number has been ground away and a new one, '110', has been over-stamped. This made it impossible to trace the weapon to any particular unit or depot after the fall of the Berlin Wall and the demise of the Warsaw Pact, when many ex-Pact weapons were being sold off to any available buyer. Media Image Photography

Barrel, muzzle brake and sight block of the East German MPiKM rifle. Unlike the MPiK, the MPiKM has the under-barrel cleaning rod permanently fitted. Media Image Photography

Detail of the MPiKM foresight post fitted with the ZVN-64 night sight. The ZVN-64 bead is in the night firing position over the foresight (it was slipped down the wire spring to allow the weapon's sight to be used during daylight). The correct night firing aim position placed the front bead above the rear bead with the target above the foresight. Media Image Photography

East German MPiKM rear sight fitted with the removable luminous ZVN-64. The ZVN-64 leaf sight is in the night firing position; it was folded down to allow the weapon's sight to be used during daylight. The luminous side bars ensured a level sight base. Media Image Photography

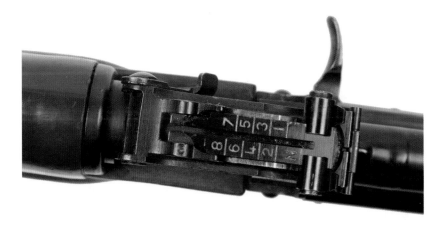

MPiKM rear sight showing graduations to 800m and the 'N' position for battle sights. Media Image Photography

A Grenztruppe (East German border guard) on the border between East and West Germany during 1969. The Grenzer is armed with an MPiKM rifle with wooden furniture. He wears Flächentarn uniform. Armeerundschau

An Iraqi soldier at Tikrit in 2004, armed with an MPiKM with full plastic furniture including the late production vertically grooved fore-end. This was just one of the many weapon types imported into Iraq. US Department of Defense

The East German MPiKMS is the side-folding stock version of the MpiKM. It uses the same receiver as the full stocked weapon, unlike under-folding stocks that require a different receiver pattern. It is often called the MPiKMS 72. Media Image Photography

East German MPiKMS with the stock folded against the right side of the receiver. The small rubber stop on the upper crutch of the shoulder stock prevents abrasion or damage to the receiver as well as reducing any noise rattle. Media Image Photography

Detail of the MPiKMS foresight post. This weapon is fitted with a blank firing adaptor. The muzzle brake is retained on the cleaning rod to prevent loss. Media Image Photography

The MPiKMS used a side-folding stock. Shown here is the stock hinge mechanism and release button fitted at the rear of the receiver. Media Image Photography

The MPiKMS side-folding stock in the extended position. Media Image Photography

Detail of the MPiKMS pistol grip and rear sling swivel. The swivel is fitted to the stock hinge mechanism and is noticeably smaller than that fitted to Russian or other nationality weapons as the NVA sling is narrower. Also visible is the rather poor quality plastic keepers used on the narrow gauge slings issued with the MPiKM and MPiKMS. Media Image Photography

The MPiKMS wood fore-end and plastic handguard. These two sections could be found in all-wood or all-plastic. Media Image Photography

'Drop bag' used by NVA Fallschirmjäger to store the MPiKMS during a parachute descent. The use of the bag made the weapon readily accessible once on the ground and helped prevent shroud lines getting tangled during the drop. Media Image Photography

An NVA Fallschirmjäger takes up a defensive position on the DZ during a training exercise. His MPiKMS is fitted with a BFA at the muzzle. The muzzle brake has been removed and, as common practice, slipped over the cleaning rod to prevent loss. Private collection

East German sling types. The late pattern sling fitted to the MPiKM rifle is typical of the low quality items in use by the NVA during much of its existence. Below is an early production sling issued with the MPiK. This sling, a direct copy of the Russian pattern, will not fit the smaller rear sling swivels found on the MPiKM and MPiKMS rifles. Media Image Photography

East German bayonet training rifle (believed to have been designated the M85). Loosely shaped to conform to the dimensions of the MPiK, it was fitted with a spring-loaded 'bayonet' with bulbous rubber tip and grooved grips. The wooden rifle lacks a pistol grip, a superfluous addition as during bayonet fighting the right hand gripped the small of the wooden stock, not the pistol grip. Media Image Photography

Early NVA magazine pouches for three 30-round magazines. At left a black leather pouch and at right a pouch made from Flächentarn camouflage fabric. At the rear of the pouches are twin belt loops and a D ring for fitting the equipment braces. Media Image Photography

At left an NVA Flächentarn magazine pouch for two 30-round magazines, and at right a four-pocket magazine pouch made from Strichtarn camouflage fabric. At the rear of the pouches are twin belt loops and a D ring for fitting the equipment braces. Also shown is an East German-manufacture 30-round magazine. Media Image Photography

East German Reinigungsgerät 57 (cleaning kit 57). The NVA cleaning kit was the most comprehensive issued by any nation. Top are the outer case with cleaning cloth, and below the inner metal case containing the cleaning kit (left to right): oil bottle, bore oil brush, bore cleaning brush (both were attached to the pull-through in use), cleaning brush, combination tools and pull-through. Media Image Photography

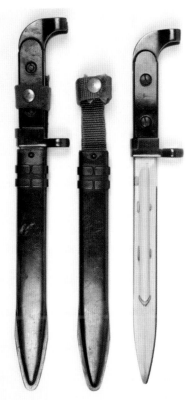

East German Modell 47 (AK) bayonets as used with the MPiK and MPiKS: (left) with a brown cotton webbing suspension hanger; (right) with a grey nylon suspension. There are a number of minor variations of scabbard design and suspension hanger colour. Media Image Photography

East German bayonets for the MPiKM and MPiKMS rifles (left to right): Modell 59 (AKM I) with black grips and rubber insulator; Modell 79 transitional bayonet (AKM I bayonet with AKM II scabbard); Modell AK74 (AKM II). The Modell AK74 was not produced until the introduction of the 5.45mm MPiAK74 so is technically not for use with MPiKM and MPiKMS rifles, although all of the AKM type bayonets were interchangeable. The Modell AK74 can also be found with orange grips. Media Image Photography

Hungary

In 1955 an agreement with the Soviet Union saw the Hungarian arms factory Fémáru Fegyver és Gépgyár (FEG) granted a licence to manufacture the AK rifle. The first domestically produced Hungarian AK rifle was made in 1959 and was called the AK55. It was a high quality copy of the type 3 receiver AK, with only minor differences including a heavily chequered pistol grip and having the weapon serial number placed in the milled cut on the left side of the receiver, rather than on the trunnion as was usual with Soviet AKs. Receiver markings were an infinity symbol (∞) for automatic and numeral '1' for single shot.

In 1963 the Hungarians turned to production of the AKM rifle. The unique AKMM63 (Automata Kalasnyikov Modernizált Magyarosított 63 – Automatic Kalashnikov Modernized Hungarian) was instantly recognizable. The AKMM63 had a distinctive design of wooden pistol grip with a flared base. Instead of the wooden gas tube handguard or fore-end usually found on AKMs, the AKMM63 had a ribbed sheet steel fore-end with integral forward pistol grip. The AKMMS63 was the folding stock version.

The AKMM63 was too long for use by troops who required a more compact weapon due to the nature of their operations. In 1965 the Hungarians tabled a requirement for a short rifle specifically for use by airborne units and paratroops. The AMD65 (Automata Modernizált Deszantfegyver 65 – Automatic Modernized Paratrooper Rifle 65) used the AKMM63 as a design base but with a side-folding stock and shortened barrel with a heavy muzzle brake/flash reducer (shortening any barrel dramatically increases muzzle flash and recoil). The AMD65 was made in large numbers and issued to a wide range of troops including AFV crews, armoured infantry and air force as well as police.

A modified AMD65 formed the design base for a grenade-launching rifle, the AMP69 (Automata Módosított Puskagránátos 69 -- Automatic Modified Grenade Launcher 69). On the AMP69 the AMD65 metal fore-end and grip were replaced by a bulbous plastic fore-end with integral spring to assist in absorbing recoil, the muzzle brake was discarded and a grenade launcher barrel extension fitted in its place. The folding stock was also modified with the addition of a shock absorber at the butt. A removable optical grenade-launching sight was fitted to the rear left of the receiver and a gas cut-off was mounted on the gas tube for use when launching grenades. A standard 30-round magazine was used with ball ammunition but for grenade launching a special short magazine was used, holding five rounds. It had a restrictor plate fitted internally, preventing the loading of ball or other bulleted ammunition.

The AKMM63 design encountered problems. It was expensive to produce and the fore grip was prone to damage. Therefore in 1977 the Hungarians undertook to make a copy of the Soviet AKM rifle without the Hungarian refinements used on the AKMM63. The AK63 (Automata Kalasnyikov 63) was a direct copy of the Soviet AKM with wooden fore-end and handguard, and using the distinctive Hungarian design for the rear pistol grip. The following year a folding stock AKMS design was added to the inventory: the fixed stock AK63 became the AK63F and the folding stock weapon was designated the AK63D. The AK63F and AK63D are also known as the AMM and AMMS, respectively. Although an AK74 type rifle was manufactured by the Hungarians, the AMM remains the standard Hungarian infantry weapon and is still used by Hungarian troops deployed to Afghanistan. On Hungarian AK63 weapons the woodwork is made of light coloured beech, giving it a quite distinct appearance.

It is believed that Hungary did not produce the AK47 bayonet but they did manufacture an AKM I type that was a close copy of the Soviet original. The Hungarian AKM I bayonet itself differed only in minor detail, most noticeably in the rounded finish of the crossguard hook (used to attach the wrist strap). The scabbard had a distinctive yellow finish rubber insulator section; this was black on the Soviet manufacture. The leather wrist strap used a buckle to secure the pommel end, rather than a riveted loop (a style also used by the Romanians). However, it was the hanger arrangement that provides for the best recognition of the Hungarian AKM I. The unique hanger has two carbine clips on the central hilt strap section. One of the clips attaches to the rear of the scabbard throat with the upper clip then fitting to the D ring of the belt loop. It is not believed that Hungary produced an AKM II bayonet. Hungarian AK slings are made from brown leather. They have the standard D ring and carbine hook at the forward end and are adjusted using a simple pronged buckle and strap fitting.

Standard Variants

AK55	Milled Type 3A receiver, fixed stock
AKMM63	Stamped Type 4A receiver, fixed stock (Hungarian variant AKM)
AKMMS63	Milled Type 3B receiver, under-folding stock (Hungarian variant AKMS)
AMD65	Stamped Type 4A receiver, side-folding stock
AMP69	Stamped Type 4A receiver, side-folding stock (AMD65 modified for grenade launching)
AK63F	Stamped Type 4A receiver, fixed stock (copy of AKM)
AK63D	Stamped Type 4B receiver, under-folding stock (copy of AKMS)

The Hungarian AK55 'Gépkarabély' was a copy of the Russian AK with the third pattern receiver. It was in production only between 1959 and 1963. Media Image Photography

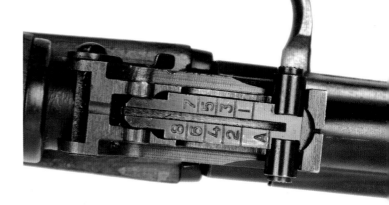

The AK55 rear sight is ranged to 1,000m with the 350m battle sight marked with an 'A'. Media Image Photography

Detail of the wooden pistol grip of the AK55. Unlike the Soviet AK, the AK55 had a chequered surface to the wooden pistol grip, providing a better grip in use. Media Image Photography

The AK55 was replaced by the AKMM63, also called the AKMM, which was essentially an AKM with a ventilated metal fore-end and front-mounted wooden pistol grip. There was no upper handguard so the gas tube was exposed. It is shown here in use by an AFV crewman who would have found the weapon's length a problem within the tight confines of an armoured vehicle. Armeerundschau

A rare picture of an AKMM63 rifle fitted with an infrared night vision lamp and sighting unit. The ventilated metal fore-end of the AKMM63 is clearly shown in this image. Armeerundschau

The Hungarian AK63F rifle, also known as the AMM, was based on the Soviet AKM and was a cheaper alternative to the indigenous AKMM63. The AK63F rifle retained the AK type handguard gas tube vents but also incorporated the gas block vents of the AKM. The AK63F has a distinctive flared base to the pistol grip. Media Image Photography

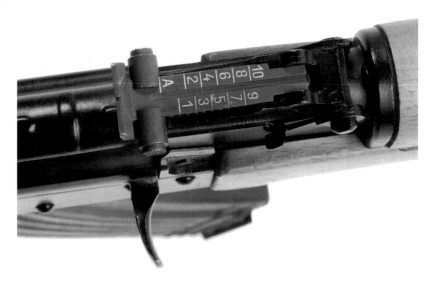

Detail of the rear sight of the AK63F. The sight has a phosphate grey finish and is ranged to 1,000m. Media Image Photography

Left side of the receiver showing the weapon's serial number M 004365 on the trunnion. Media Image Photography

An Iraqi National Guard soldier on a joint security patrol outside the city of Baqubah, Iraq, during 2004. He is armed with a Hungarian AK63F rifle with typically light beech woodwork. US Department of Defense

An Iraqi police officer demonstrates the disassembly of the AK63F, Mosul, Iraq, 2009. The receiver cover and working parts have been removed and the officer is lifting the gas tube lever, prior to removal of the handguard and gas tube. US Department of Defense

Left side of the AK63D based on the AKMS (also known as the AKS63 or AMMS), with the stock folded under the receiver. The under-folding stock is the standard Soviet pattern. Media Image Photography

Left side of the AK63D showing the stamped steel under-folding stock in the extended position. Media Image Photography

Rear sight block, trunnion and front of the receiver of the AK63D showing the lack of any markings other than the serial number. Media Image Photography

AK63D rear sight. Ranged to 1,000m, the battle sight setting is marked by an 'A'. Media Image Photography

AK63D barrel, muzzle brake and foresight post. All conform to the standard AKM pattern. Media Image Photography

The main identifying feature of Hungarian AK63 type weapons is the distinctive beech wood pistol grip with flared base, providing a firmer hold. The grip illustrated is fitted to an AK63D, as shown by the folding stock. Media Image Photography

A Hungarian soldier on field exercise during 2006. He is armed with a folding stock AK63D rifle fitted with a blank firing adaptor. It has the Hungarian pattern of leather sling. Hungarian Defence Ministry

One of the most distinctive of all Hungarian AKM type weapons is the AMD65 (Automata Modernizált Deszant). The gun has a ventilated steel fore-end without a handguard over the gas tube (similar to that used on the AKM63), a vertical fore grip, shortened barrel and a characteristic bulbous flash eliminator (necessitated by the reduced barrel length). Media Image Photography

The AMD65 with the simple single strut side-folding stock closed against the right side. When folded the stock did not interfere with the selector lever. The plastic pistol grips can be found in a variety of shades from black to grey and a distinctive pale blue. Beech wood grips were also used but are less common than the plastic type. Media Image Photography

Detail of the AMD65 sight block, trunnion and receiver, showing a section of the ventilated fore-end. The AMD65 was a shortened version of the AKMM63 for use by specialist troops requiring a smaller weapon. Media Image Photography

Right side of the AMD65's receiver showing the selector lever and markings, an infinity symbol (∞) for automatic and a numeral '1' for single shot. Media Image Photography

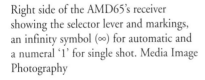

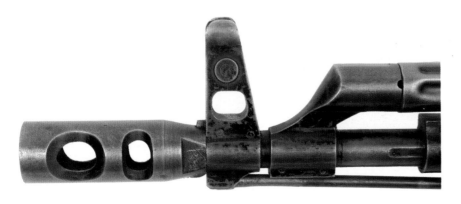

Detail of the foresight post and flash eliminator of the AMD65. The weapon had no provision for the fitting of a bayonet. The compact size of the weapon made it ideal for units requiring a short weapon, such as AFV crews and special forces. Media Image Photography

The brown leather sling used on Hungarian weapons was quite distinctive as it used a pronged roller buckle arrangement for adjustment, rather than the commonly encountered tension buckle. At top is a Hungarian sling fitted to an AMD65, below is a second sling showing the arrangement of buckle and carbine hook. Media Image Photography

A fine study of an Afghan National Police officer in Keshem, Afghanistan, January 2009. He carries an AMD65 with wooden pistol grips. Of note is the split ring that has been threaded through the cleaning rod end, improving ease of removal and use. ISAF Media

To further reduce the overall length of the AMD65, the mechanism of the folding stock was inset into the rear of the receiver. It was operated by a press catch located on the underside of the weapon, behind the rear pistol grip. Media Image Photography

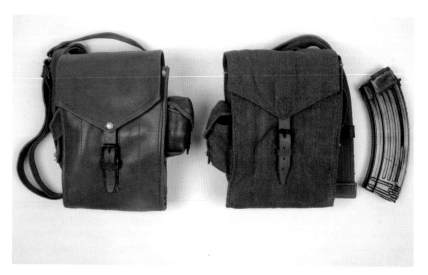

Typical Hungarian magazine pouches. Both hold five 30-round magazines, have shoulder straps and twin belt loops at the rear. At left, a waterproof green plastic pouch with leather shoulder strap; at right, a lightweight canvas pouch with webbing shoulder strap. External pockets hold the combination tool and oil bottle (not shown). At far right is a Hungarian-manufacture 30-round magazine. Media Image Photography

The AMD65 folding stock in the extended position. It was a simple and effective design that incorporated a rubber butt. Media Image Photography

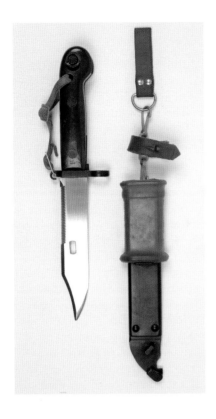

Hungarian AKM I type bayonet. Hungarian manufacture bayonets can be identified by the unique hanger that has two carbine clips on the central strap section. One clip attaches to the belt loop and one to the scabbard throat. Media Image Photography

While AKM type weapons are usually sighted to an unrealistic 1,000m, the AMD65 rear sight is ranged to a mere 800m, as used on the original AK weapon types. Media Image Photography

The AMD65 vertical fore grip. A vertical grip had first been used on the AKM63. Media Image Photography

Hungarian four-pocket pouch to hold 20-round magazines. This black pouch was issued to police units and used with the AMD65 rifle. It has two belt loops on the rear and external pockets to hold the combination tool and oil bottles. At right are a Hungarian 20-round magazine, AMD65 muzzle wrench, combination tool, and a holder for cleaning solvent and oil bottles. A similar pouch for 20-round magazines was made of canvas or green plastic for use by Army units requiring a low-capacity magazine. Media Image Photography

Iraq

Iraq began the manufacture of a Kalashnikov in the early 1980s, prior to which it had imported a wide variety of AK type weapons. The new Iraqi weapon was named after the ancient battle of Tabuk (AD 630). The Tabuk was produced on machinery and expertise imported from Yugoslavia and was a close copy of the Yugoslav M70. It is believed that the earlier weapons had no grenade launcher but this was incorporated on later production weapons. The Tabuk was produced with both fixed and folding stocks but it would appear that there was no sub-classification of the two types other than the suffix 'wooden' or 'folding stock'. A short version of the folding stock Tabuk was also manufactured. It had an overall length of 80cm with stock extended, compared to the 89cm of the standard folding stock Tabuk or the 90cm of the wood stock version. It was marketed as the Tabuk short assault rifle. A multitude of custom-made Tabuk rifles were manufactured to meet the demands of well-heeled Iraqi officials and others who had a requirement for self-protection or prestige weapons. The Iraqi Arab culture produced a market for weapons showing individual status. This was fed by a variety of AK type weapons personalized to individual taste or to meet market demands, including gold- or chrome-plated weapons and ornate, often quite gaudy, grips, fore-end and handguards.

Iraq also produced a variant of the Tabuk rifle based on the standard M70 style receiver, but without the usual trunnion bulge. Again it was made with a fixed or folding stock and had the Yugoslav style fore-end and handguard.

The long three-vent handguards and fore-ends fitted to the Tabuk were not interchangeable with those of the standard AK or AKM, nor was the receiver cover, which was approximately a centimetre shorter than the standard AK or AKM pattern. The rear sight was also set back slightly further on the Tabuk, giving the Iraqi rifle a sight base of 393mm on the grenade-launching Tabuk rifle or 388mm on the Tabuk without grenade launcher, compared to 377mm on the AK and 380mm on the AKM.

Domestic weapon production was never sufficient to meet demand and Iraq continued to import weapons for its armed forces. AK type weapons from China, Romania and East Germany as well as Hungary were used in the conflict against Iran and later during the Gulf War.

Iraq imported many AKM bayonets, mainly Russian, Hungarian and Romanian, along with thousands of Romanian bayonet frogs. An indigenous AKM II bayonet was also produced by Iraqi manufacturers. The earliest production was an AKM II bayonet with an AKM I scabbard assembly (a combination often referred to as the Transitional AKM I). This was later upgraded to an AKM II bayonet and AKM II scabbard produced in a distinctive orange plastic, similar to Russian production. While serving in Iraq the author observed several Iraqi production bayonets that had broken blades, fracturing across the wire-cutter lug recess – an obvious weak point on any blade but one that was perhaps unduly so on some AKM bayonets.

Iraqi weapons can be found with a multitude of sling types, ranging from imported Polish, Chinese and other manufacture to indigenous production of somewhat diverse quality. They were often kept in use far beyond their effective life.

An early production Iraqi Tabuk rifle. Based on the Yugoslav M70B1, it lacks the grenade launcher and night sights, and has a Bulgarian style pistol grip. It is marked 'Tabuk Cal 7.62×39mm' on the right side of the sight block. Like the M70B1, the gas tube handguard has three vent holes rather than the usual two and the wooden stock has a rubber base. As well as the M70B1 style receiver, a variant of the Tabuk rifle was also produced with an AKM style receiver without the trunnion bulges. Media Image Photography

Left side of the early production Tabuk rifle showing that it has been cut away as an armourer's demonstration model. Note the sling swivel fitted to the rear of the receiver, as on AK variants, rather than on the wood stock as is usual for fully stocked AKM type weapons. The cutaway magazine, showing the rounds and magazine follower, is originally of Chinese manufacture. Media Image Photography

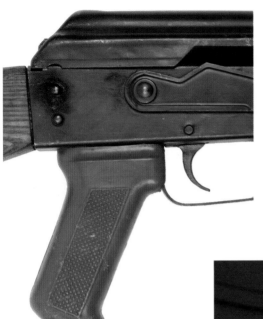

Right side of the early production Tabuk rifle receiver showing the selector lever and Arabic selector markings. Media Image Photography

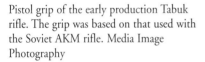

Pistol grip of the early production Tabuk rifle. The grip was based on that used with the Soviet AKM rifle. Media Image Photography

Souped-up early pattern Tabuk rifle (non-grenade launcher) with fitted side rail for a telescopic sight, removable forward pistol grip and a tactical light held on by a bandage. It is fitted with a Chinese 20-round magazine. The weapon was being used by an Iraqi soldier during a raid conducted in Sadr City, Baghdad, during 2005. US Department of Defense

Standard pattern Iraqi Tabuk rifle with grenade launcher fitted and launching sight raised. This rifle is a direct copy of the Yugoslav M70B1. Like the M70 type weapons, the Tabuk handguard and fore-end have three ventilation holes as opposed to the two found on most AKs. At the rear of the receiver below the cover is the reverse of the press catch that locked the recoil spring guide in place and prevented the receiver cover from being dislodged by the shock of grenade discharge. Media Image Photography

Tabuk rifle rear sight ranged to 1,000m, with a battle sight setting marked by a '0'. The integral luminous night sight is in the day (folded down) position. Media Image Photography

Tabuk rifle with grenade launching sight raised. Raising the sight cuts off the gas flow through the gas block to the gas piston. This prevents the action cycling but ensures that all propellant gases are fed through to the launcher. Media Image Photography

Right side of the sight block showing the 'Tabuk Cal 7.62×39mm' marking. Media Image Photography

Left side of the sight block showing the Tabuk weapon designation and calibre in Arabic script and the Asad Babil (Lion of Babylon) marking applied to all Tabuk rifles made at the state arms factory. The factory, located near Bi'r Musammad in Babylon Province, was destroyed by US forces in 2003. Media Image Photography

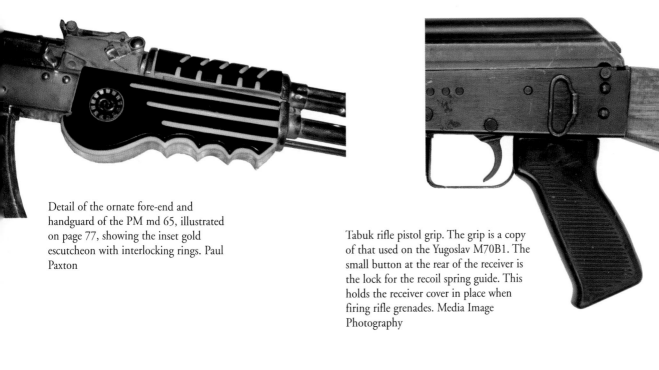

Detail of the ornate fore-end and handguard of the PM md 65, illustrated on page 77, showing the inset gold escutcheon with interlocking rings. Paul Paxton

Tabuk rifle pistol grip. The grip is a copy of that used on the Yugoslav M70B1. The small button at the rear of the receiver is the lock for the recoil spring guide. This holds the receiver cover in place when firing rifle grenades. Media Image Photography

A unique Iraqi variant of the AKM with a stubby barrel is known as the Tabuk Short Assault Rifle. The weapon is a standard Tabuk with AKM type receiver and folding stock fitted with red plastic fore-end and handguard. The right side of the sight block bears the standard 'Tabuk Cal 7.62×39mm' marking. The Tabuk SAR has a unique short barrel with a combined foresight and gas block; with the stock folded it is a mere 555mm (22in) in length. There is no provision for the fitting of a bayonet or a cleaning rod. Paul Paxton

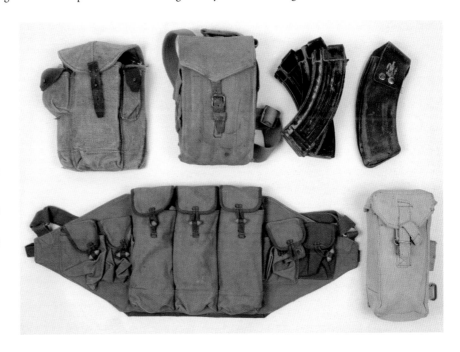

Magazine pouch types used by Iraqi forces during the Gulf War of 1991: (top, left to right) a Russian pattern three-pocket pouch, a Hungarian type four-magazine pouch with three rather dirty magazines found with the Hungarian pouch, two of which bear the Russian Izhmash 'arrow in triangle' logo; at right is a leather single-magazine pouch marked with the Iraqi army's eagle insignia on the top flap. Below is a Chinese pattern chest rig and at right a Chinese-made P58 webbing pouch, the left side of a pair, which was able to hold three magazines. Media Image Photography

An interesting weapons cache found by US Marines during 2003. At left is what appears to be a chromed East German MPiKMS with Russian pattern woodwork. The accompanying chromed magazine is of the Chinese pattern. At right is a Tabuk Short Assault Rifle (SAR). US Department of Defense

Folding stock Tabuk rifle based on the Yugoslav M70AB2. The rifle is carried by an Iraqi police officer providing security at a police training complex in southern Iraq. Author's photograph

Gas block and foresight post on the early Tabuk rifle. The gas block has a distinctive form and is based on that of the M70B1 but without the grenade sight or gas stop valve. An Iraqi-made AKM II bayonet is fitted to the muzzle. Media Image Photography

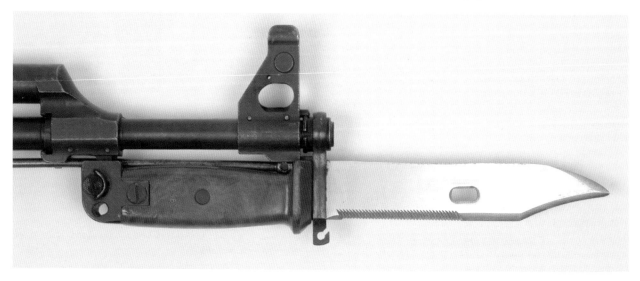

A group of Iraqi police patrol the Meshra al Bawi area of Baghdad, 2007. The officer at left carries a highly unusual Tabuk variant. It appears to be a hybrid of the folding stock Tabuk based on the Russian AKSU (a 5.56×45mm weapon). It has the flip-up receiver cover of the AKSU (hinged at the front) but the rear sight is located further back on the receiver cover (giving a longer sight base). It has an unusual gas block and foresight but unfortunately the muzzle is hidden. US Department of Defense

An American tracked vehicle destroys captured weapons during Operation *Iraqi Freedom* in 2003. Allied forces went to great lengths to destroy Iraqi weaponry, so much so that AK type weapons were later in such short supply that pattern types needed to be bought from foreign suppliers in order to equip the re-formed Iraqi security forces. A variety of AK types are visible, including a large number of Chinese Type 56 rifles; surprisingly at least two SMLE rifles can also be seen in the top right of the image. US Department of Defense

This highly ornamental AKMS started life as an export version of the Romanian PM md 65, many of which were imported for use by the Iraqi military. The metalwork has been polished and plated and the original wooden pistol grip, fore-end and handguard have been replaced by an ornate black and white layered composite material. Gold- and chrome-plated weapons were popular status symbols among the higher echelons of Iraqi society. Paul Paxton

North Korea (Democratic People's Republic of)

North Korea had an uneasy alliance with the Soviet Union and China, both of whom had supplied arms and equipment during the Korean War. By 1958 agreement had been reached to produce the Russian AK rifle in North Korea. With Soviet assistance production of the indigenous Type 58 rifle was soon underway. This was a copy of the third pattern receiver AK, produced in both fixed Type 58A and folding stock Type 58B variants.

Some 800,000 Type 58 rifles were produced before production was switched to a stamped receiver AKM type weapon designated the Type 68. The new weapon retained the old AK style smooth receiver cover and flat muzzle nut; again it was produced in both fixed Type 68A and folding stock Type 68B variants.

Both the Type 58 and Type 68 weapon types are still in service with military reserve forces, the Workers' and Peasants' Red Guard and the Young Red Guard. According to DPRK sources, their version of the AK rifle is the best in the world.

While the Type 58 rifle was provided with a copy of the Soviet AK47 bayonet, the Type 68 rifle used a bayonet that was unique to North Korea. At first glance it appears quite similar to the AK47 bayonet but it is a very distinctive design. It uses an inverted clip-point blade with fullers, plastic grip scales and a distinctive rounded pommel not dissimilar to that used on the AK47 bayonet. The same pattern of scabbard was used on both the Type 58 and Type 68 bayonets.

Standard Variants

Type 58A	Type 3A receiver, fixed stock
Type 58B	Type 3B receiver, under-folding stock
Type 68A	Type 4A receiver, fixed stock
Type 68B	Type 4B receiver, under-folding stock

Right side of a Type 58 rifle, a copy of the Soviet type 3 milled receiver AK produced in North Korea between 1958 and 1968. The Soviet foresight post is standard on the Type 58 but examples fitted with a Chinese pattern closed top sight post have been noted. Media Image Photography

Left side of the North Korean Type 58 rifle. Other than the markings, and perhaps the distinctive Catalpa wood furniture, there is little to distinguish it from a Soviet type 3 receiver AK. Media Image Photography

Left side of the receiver of the Type 58 showing the North Korean property stamp of a star within a circle and the poorly stamped serial number. A mismatched serial is stamped on the receiver cover. Media Image Photography

Right side of the receiver of the Type 58 showing the selector lever and Korean Hangul characters for automatic and single shot settings. The milled section has quite a rough finish compared to Soviet AK rifles. Media Image Photography

Type 58 rifle rear sight ranged to 800m
with Hangul character showing the battle
sight setting. Media Image Photography

The Type 58 rifle's pistol grip and rear
receiver, showing the sling attachment
point. Media Image Photography

A Korean People's Army Lance Corporal stands guard near the DMZ. He is armed with the Type 68 rifle, the North Korean version of the AKM. The rear sling swivel attachment is fitted to the receiver in the manner of the Type 58 and as standard on AK patterns, unlike other AKM full stock variants that have the rear swivel on the stock itself. The weapon is fitted with the Type 68 bayonet. Private collection

North Korean Type 68 bayonet. The Type 58 rifle used a standard AK bayonet based on the Soviet pattern. However, the Type 68 rifle had a bayonet that was unique to North Korea. At first glance it appears similar to the AK bayonet but, although the scabbard is almost identical, the bayonet has a clip-point bowie style blade and an AKM style crosspiece and pommel fixing catch. The blade style has also been noted on a rare variant of the North Korean Type 58 bayonet, but it is not known if this blade design preceded the Type 68 rifle or if it was a retrospective upgrade used on post-1968 production Type 58 bayonets. Media Image Photography

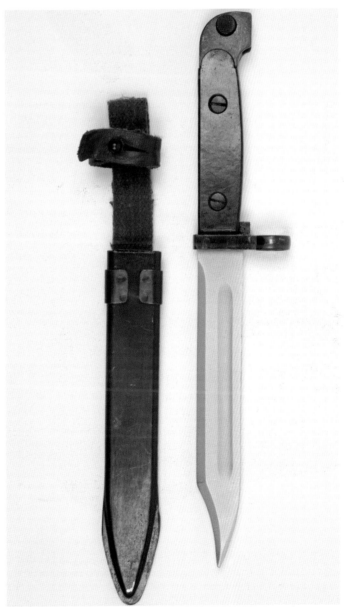

Pakistan

The nation that is now Pakistan (prior to 1947 it was a part of India under British rule) has a long history of copying weapons. During the eighteenth and nineteenth centuries hand-made copies of British military long arms, particularly the Martini Henry and SMLE, were produced in the tribal Khyber Pass border area between Pakistan and Afghanistan. Modern Pakistan has its own state arms factories producing a variety of weapon types, including Kalashnikov copies produced as the PK10 assault rifle. The PK10 has been harshly criticized by Russian delegations as a breach of rights, but the Pakistanis have always insisted the rights were licensed from China.

The most ubiquitous Kalashnikovs to be found in Pakistan are undoubtedly the Khyber Pass copies. These are predominantly AKM type weapons, more often than not sporting an AKS74 style triangular skeleton stock. They can be rather poor in finish with obvious machining and poorly scribed markings copied from genuine weapons. Some show exceptionally fine workmanship, but even the best rarely stand up to close scrutiny or direct comparison with genuine weapons.

The border region of the Khyber Pass, between Pakistan and Afghanistan, has always had a thriving arms industry. Local craftsmen are famed for their ability to produce almost any weapon with only the most rudimentary of tools. Usually vaunted as indiscernible from the original weapons, close scrutiny often reveals their true origin. This weapon, photographed in Afghanistan following capture from Taliban forces, is typical of the locally produced weapon type. It appears to be an Egyptian Misr rifle modified by the addition of an AKS74 style folding stock. However, close inspection reveals numerous small details that point to its true origin. WO Ed Storey, CEFCOM HQ

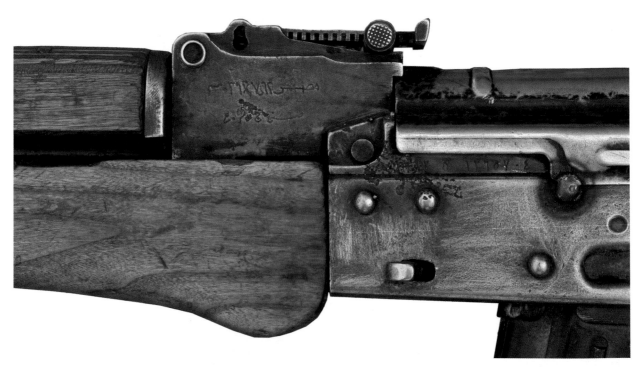

The 'Khyber Pass' weapon even has typical Misr sight block markings and a trunnion serial number preceded by the Maadi logo. These differ slightly in style from the original Egyptian markings. This example has the receiver cover spot welded to the receiver, making it virtually impossible to clean the working parts. Afghan weapons can also be found with the magazine welded in position, necessitating awkward single round reloading through the ejection port. WO Ed Storey, CEFCOM HQ

A second 'Khyber Pass' made AKM rifle, this time a stubby version with reduced barrel length (some 12cm shorter than a standard AKM) and a typical AKS74 folding stock. It was part of a haul recovered by Canadian forces in Afghanistan and is being displayed by WO Ed Storey, CEFCOM HQ war diarist, during Operation *Keepsake*. WO Ed Storey, CEFCOM HQ

Poland

Poland began licensed manufacture of the Soviet AK rifle with the type 3 receiver in the late 1950s. The Polish production AK was called the PMK (Pistolet Maszynowy Kalasznikowa – Kalashnikov Submachine Gun); the AKS folding stock variant was known as the PMKS (Pistolet Maszynowy Kalasznikowa Skladany – Kalashnikov Submachine Gun Folding). This type of weapon would not have been designated a submachine gun in western circles, so the terminology can be confusing to many. During the 1970s the PMK and PMKS were redesignated the Kbk AK (Karabinek Automatyczny Kalasznikowa – Kalashnikov Automatic Carbine) and Kbk AKS (Karabinek Automatyczny Kalasznikowa Skladany).

The type 4 stamped receiver AKM went into production in Poland as the PMKM (Pistolet Maszynowy Kalasznikowa Modernizowany – Modernized Kalashnikov Submachine Gun), soon followed by the folding stock PMKMS (Pistolet Maszynowy Kalasznikowa Modernizowany Skladany). As with the AK type PMK rifles, the PMKM and PMKS also underwent a change in designation during the 1970s. The PMKM became the Kbk AKM (Karabinek Automatyczny Kalasznikowa Modernizowany – Modernized Kalashnikov Automatic Carbine) and the PMKMS was redesignated the Kbk AKMS (Karabinek Automatyczny Kalasznikowa Modernizowany Skladany). The Kbk carbine prefix is often left off in Polish publications.

Polish Kalashnikov weapons were produced at the Radom factory of Zaklady Metalowe im. gen. Waltera (General Walter's Metal Plant) and bear the distinctive logo of an '11' within an oval cartouche, which had been introduced in 1950. Previous to World War II the factory had been called Zaklady Metalowe Lucznik (Metal Works Lucznik) and it reverted to that name in 1990.

Poland produced its own versions of the AK, AKM I and AKM II bayonets. All are quite distinct and differ from the Soviet originals in detail. The AK bayonet is a direct copy of the Russian type, usually marked on the crossguard with the 'oval 11' logo and the date. The scabbard is quite different from Russian manufacture. It lacks the pressed seam at the tip, common to most AK47 bayonet scabbards, and it has a unique leather frog fitted using a short leather tab and two wire loops on the rear of the scabbard. This allows it to be easily removed for repair or replacement. The Polish variant of the AKM I bayonet was designated the Bagnetu Wz. 6H3. It was a close copy of the Soviet AKM I but lacked the serrated saw teeth to the back of the blade. The Polish AKM II was designated the Bagnetu Wz. 6H4. Like the 6H3, the 6H4 also had a plain blade without saw teeth. The scabbard type used with both the 6H3 and 6H4 was of the AKM I pattern.

An unusual spring-loaded training (fencing) bayonet was also made by the Poles. It was based on the 6H4 hilt with a flat blade having a bulbous rubber tip. The blade could be pushed into the hilt when pressure was applied to the tip. For storage the blade could be retracted and locked into the hilt using a catch located at the crossguard. The fencing bayonet was designated the Wz.85 Gall. These bayonets bear the Radom 'oval 11' mark and the year of manufacture on the pommel (commonly dated between 1985 and 1988).

Polish Kalashnikov slings follow the standard Russian pattern and are produced in cotton or nylon webbing ranging in colour from tan to green.

Standard Variants

PMK (Kbk Ak)	Type 3A receiver, fixed stock
PMKS (Kbk AKS)	Type 3B receiver under-folding stock
PMK PGN60 (Kbk Ak PGN60)	Type 3A receiver, fixed stock (grenade launching variant)
PMKM (Kbk AKM)	Type 4A receiver, fixed stock
PMKMS (Kbk AKMS)	Type 4B receiver, under-folding stock

Polish Kbk AKS (Karabinek Automatyczny Kalasznikowa Skladany), originally known as the PMKS (Pistolet Maszynowy Kalasznikowa Skladany). This is the folding stock version of the standard Kbk AK rifle. Of exceptionally high quality, it differs little from the Russian AKS. Weapon courtesy PDH Enterprises

Iraqi paratroops parade with Polish Kbk AK riles with fixed bayonets at Al Muthana Air Base, Iraq, 2009. US Department of Defense

The armoury at Basra police station photographed during 2005. The Iraqi police officer holds a Polish Kbk AK rifle (Karabinek Automatyczny Kalasznikowa, originally known as the PMK – Pistolet Maszynowy Kalasznikowa), with others mounted on the wall to the right. All have the green nylon Polish type slings. The wall behind holds a selection of war-weary Chinese stamped receiver Type 56 rifles. Author's photograph

Polish Kbk AKS rifle with the under-folding stock in the closed position. The Soviet pattern under-folding stock was used by most AK weapon-producing nations. However, in the folded position it did hinder use of the selector lever, particularly when attempting to select the automatic or single shot positions. The inner face of the stock's right arm was cut away at the point where the selector lever passed under it, but it was still difficult to use the selector with the stock folded. Weapon courtesy PDH Enterprises

Right side receiver of the Polish Kbk AKS rifle showing selector lever and markings of 'C' (Ciagly) and 'P' (Pojedynczy) for automatic and single shot fire. The diamond-shaped stamp in the milled-out section of the receiver is an inspector's marking. Weapon courtesy PDH Enterprises

The left side of the Polish Kbk AKS rifle with stock folded. Weapon courtesy PDH Enterprises

Detail of the left side of the Kbk AKS receiver showing the Fabryka Broni Lucznik (Radom) factory marking of an '11' within an oval, the year of manufacture 1962 and the weapon serial number. Weapon courtesy PDH Enterprises

Right side of the Polish Kbk AKMS (Karabinek Automatyczny Kalasznikowa Modernizowany Skladany) with stock extended. This was originally known as the PMKMS (Pistolet Maszynowy Kalasznikowa Modernizowany Skladany). Media Image Photography

Left side of the Kbk AKMS with the stock folded. Media Image Photography

The Kbk AKMS stamped steel folding stock in the extended position. Media Image Photography

Kbk AKMS selector lever showing the 'C' (Ciagly) and 'P' (Pojedynczy) for automatic and single shot fire. The safe position, as set on this weapon, was not marked. Media Image Photography

Forward left side of the Kbk AKMS receiver showing the trunnion marking consisting of the Radom 'oval 11' stamp, 1979 date and serial number. Media Image Photography

Rear sight of the Kbk AKMS rifle, graduated to 1,000m with an 'S' for the 350m battle setting. Media Image Photography

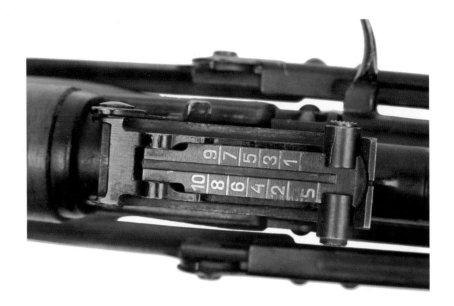

Detail of the grip and rear sling swivel (integral to the folding stock hinge) of the Polish Kbk AKMS rifle. Media Image Photography

A Polish Sierzant (Sergeant) photographed on a joint exercise held in the USA during 1979. He carries a Kbk AKMS fitted with Multiple Integrated Laser Engagement System (MILES). Of note are the three magazines taped together for quick magazine changes. The drawback of such practice is that the open top of the magazine, particularly the inverted one, is open to the ingress of dirt, which can lead to mis-feeding of the rounds. US Department of Defense

Polish bayonets. At left is the AK style bayonet as used with the Kbk AK and Kbk AKS rifles. The scabbard differs from the Soviet pattern AK bayonet in that it does not have the flat welded section at the tip, and the distinctive pattern leather hanger is easily removable. The bayonet bears the 'oval 11' marking on the left crossguard and the date 1958 on the right. At right is the 6H4 (AKM II) bayonet, a close copy of the Soviet pattern bayonet; the Polish blades lack the saw-tooth serrations. The Poles retained the AKM I style of scabbard with the 6H4. The Polish 6H3 (AKM I) bayonet is not illustrated: apart from the lack of blade serrations it was a copy of the Soviet AKM I. Media Image Photography

Polish Wz 74 Pallad 40mm under-slung grenade launcher. This weapon entered service in 1974 and was designed for use with the PMKM (Kbk AKM) rifle. Shown here is the left side with the sight and ranging drum. At the launcher's breech end is the safety, set to the fire position of a white 'O'. To engage safe 'Z', a small serrated catch (to the left of the 'Z' mark) has to be depressed before sliding the safety catch lever forward to the red 'Z' safe marking. The plastic fore-end is an integral component of the Pallad and is essential for fitting the launcher to the rifle. The rear of the launcher is held on the rifle by the plastic fore-end and the front of the launcher is clamped to the bayonet lug. Media Image Photography

The Poles manufactured a quite unique pattern of training or 'fencing' bayonet. The Wz85 (Wzor 85 – model 85) used a 6H4 hilt with a spring-retracted flat blade with bulbous rubber tip. When the bayonet was thrust into an opponent, hand-held or mounted on the rifle, the blade retracted into the hilt. The blade could be locked in the retracted position and released by means of a small button at the base of the blade below the crossguard. At left is the Wz85 with blade extended and at right it is retracted and locked into the hilt. Media Image Photography

Polish Wz 74 Pallad 40mm under-slung grenade launcher. Shown here is the right side of the launcher with the breech operating lever and trigger, which is a simple push button located forward of and just below the breech release lever. Media Image Photography

The breech of the Wz 74 Pallad shown in the open position ready for loading the 40mm grenade. Although the system operates adequately with the standard 30-round magazine fitted, the arrangement is quite a snug fit. When the Wz 74 is fitted to the PMKMS (Kbk AKMS) rifle the folding stock cannot be fully closed as it rests against the breech of the launcher. Media Image Photography

Polish nylon webbing rifle slings. A green hue sling fitted to a Kbk AKS with a brown sling laid below for comparison. Media Image Photography

Detail of the range drum quadrant of the Wz 74 Pallad 40mm grenade launcher. The launcher is ranged from 0 to 430m for direct observed fire (as shown here the sight is set at 400m direct observed fire). The ranges to the left of this setting, as viewed, are 170 to 430m indirect fire. Indirect fire is a high-angle launch for use from behind cover or when entrenched. Media Image Photography

Typical Polish three-pocket 30-round magazine ammunition pouch. It has an external pocket for the combination tool. At right is a Polish-made thirty round magazine. Media Image Photography

Romania

During the late 1950s Romania imported Soviet-made AK rifles to provide its army with a modern weapon and maintain Warsaw Pact weapons cohesion. It was not until the early 1960s that Romania began production of its own Kalashnikov rifle. The Pistolul Mitraliera model 1963 (PM md 63 – Machine Gun model 1963) was a full-stocked assault rifle based on the Soviet stamped receiver AKM. The Romanian weapon was quite distinct in appearance as the fore-end had an integral vertical pistol grip (foregrip) with a forward curve. The Romanians felt that this grip reduced the vertical muzzle climb and improved weapon accuracy in full automatic fire. Other than the Hungarians, no other manufacturing nation felt the need for a vertical foregrip. A special version of the PM md 63 was issued to the Garzile Patriotice (Patriotic Guard), a home defence unit. These weapons were converted to fire single shot with no provision for full automatic fire. To differentiate them from standard weapons, a large 'G' (representing Garzile) was engraved on the left side of the sight block.

In 1965 the Romanians developed a folding stock version of the PM md 63, designated the PM md 65. The under-folding stock of the PM md 65 was not compatible with the forward curved pistol grip of the PM md 63, so a modified grip was designed with a rearward curve that allowed the stock to fold without interference. As with all of the under-folding stock designs, it required a different receiver than that of the full stock weapon. The PM md 63 and PM md 65 were widely exported as the AIM and AIMS, respectively.

Taking the lead from East Germany, the Romanians replaced the PM md 65 with a weapon having a side-folding stock based on that used with the MpiKMS. This allowed both the full wooden stock and folding stock rifles to be built on the same PM md 63 type receiver, saving time and money. The new side-folding weapon was designated the PM md 90. As the fore-end grip shape was not an issue with the side-folding stock, the grip had a forward curve as found on the PM md 63.

Romania did not produce an AK47 bayonet but they did manufacture both the AKM I and AKM II variants. The AKM I can usually be identified as Romanian by the serial numbers with the letters prefix etched on the crossguard and scabbard face (typically two or three letters with a space and four numbers). The wrist strap of brown leather had a three-slot buckle for attachment to the crossguard and a standard friction buckle for the hilt fitting.

Romanian AKM I scabbard insulators were normally a light grey or tan colour, the scabbard type being retained for use on the AKM II bayonets. This was necessitated by the Romanians' use of a bayonet frog, rather than a hanger strap, for suspension from the equipment. The frogs had a broad leather strap that fitted around the insulator section of the scabbard using a post-and-slot fitting. Early frogs were made of leather, usually stained black for use by the Fortele Aeriene Romane (Air Force). Later production frogs were of webbing with leather for both the scabbard body and bayonet hilt straps.

Romanian Kalashnikov slings were of russet brown leather and a straight copy of the standard Russian pattern. A heavy weave green nylon webbing sling was later produced and can occasionally be found with 7.62mm weapons.

Standard Variants

PM md 63	Type 4A receiver, fixed stock (MD63)
PM md 65 (MD65)	Type 4B receiver, under-folding stock
PM md 90	Type 4A receiver, side-folding stock

The Romanian AKM was designated the Pistol Mitraliera model 63. The stamped receiver PM md 63 rifle was the first AK to be made in Romania. It has a distinctive vertical foregrip that readily identifies Romanian AK weapons. The PM md 63 is also known as the MD63. Media Image Photography

Left side receiver markings of the PM md 63 showing the year of manufacture as 1988 and the serial number. This weapon was made at the Cugir plant, which exported weapons to many nations worldwide. Media Image Photography

PM md 63 rear sight graduated from 100 to 1,000m with the battle sight position marked with a 'P'. Media Image Photography

Selector lever on a Romanian-issue PM md 63. Indigenous weapons were marked 'S' ('Sigur', safe), 'FA' ('Foc Automat', automatic) and 'FF' ('Foc cu Foc') for single shot. Media Image Photography

A Romanian airman stands guard at Craiova Air Base. He is armed with the PM md 63 rifle with fixed bayonet. The bayonet scabbard is suspended from the belt with a typically Romanian style black leather frog. A black leather magazine pouch is also just visible worn on the right side. US Department of Defense

The Romanian version of the AKMS was designated the PM md 65. It used a Soviet pattern under-folding stock that necessitated a redesign of the foregrip. To allow the stock to be folded closed, the grip was angled rearward. The PM md 65 is also known as the MD65. Media Image Photography

The foregrip, an integral part of the fore-end of the Romanian PM md 63, showing the forward curve of the grip used on this full stocked weapon. Media Image Photography

Left side of the PM md 65 with the stock folded, showing how it lays against the foregrip. The standard forward curved grip style would prevent the stock from folding fully. Media Image Photography

The foregrip of the Romanian PM md 65, showing the rearward curve of the grip necessitated by the under-folding stock, which is shown in the folded position. Media Image Photography

The folding stock of the PM md 65 in the extended position. Media Image Photography

Romanian PM md 65 selector markings on weapons produced for export were 'S', 'A' and 'R' for safe, single and automatic fire. Media Image Photography

Trunnion markings on an export PM md 65 showing the serial number AK 5589. Media Image Photography

The foresight and gas block of the PM md 65 are faithful to the original Soviet AKM design. Media Image Photography

A Romanian infantry captain at Bucharest airport, December 1989. Armed with a PM md 65, he gives a 'V' victory sign following the overthrow of the Ceausescu regime. His communist cap badge has been removed. US Department of Defense

The Romanian PM was also made with a side-folding stock, based on that used with the East German MPiKMS. The PM md 90 used the forward curved foregrip of the PM md 63 as it did not interfere with the side-folding mechanism. The PM md 90 is also known as the MD90. Media Image Photography

Right side of the PM md 90 with the stock folded against the receiver. This weapon was used in the Balkan conflict and has typical graffiti on the woodwork and pistol grip. It is fitted with a Yugoslav-made magazine. Media Image Photography

Left side of the PM md 90 with stock folded. The weapon serial number SZ 4290 is stamped on the trunnion. Media Image Photography

The rear pistol grip of the PM md 65, made from red plastic. This style of pistol grip is used on all Romanian weapons. Media Image Photography

Rear of the PM md 90 showing the press catch and stock folding mechanism. The rear of the receiver cover is marked with the weapon serial number SZ 4290. Media Image Photography

PM md 90 side-folding stock in the extended position. The stock is quite sturdy and fits to the standard type 4 receiver used on the PM md 63 rifle. Media Image Photography

Romanian PM md 63 rifle fitted with standard Romanian brown leather sling. Below are the leather sling and a late production green webbing sling. Media Image Photography

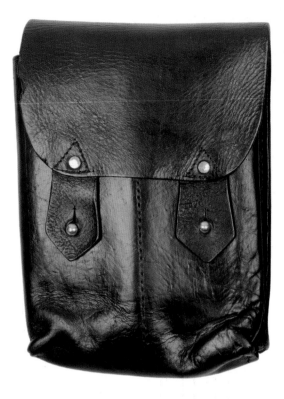 

Romanian leather magazine pouches. The pouches hold four 30-round magazines. At left is a black pouch used by the Air Force and at right a brown pouch as used by the Army. The rear of the pouch has two loops for suspension from the belt. Media Image Photography

Romanian canvas magazine pouches. The pouch at left holds four 30-round magazines, while the one at right has pockets for three magazines. External pockets hold the cleaning kit and oil bottle. Media Image Photography

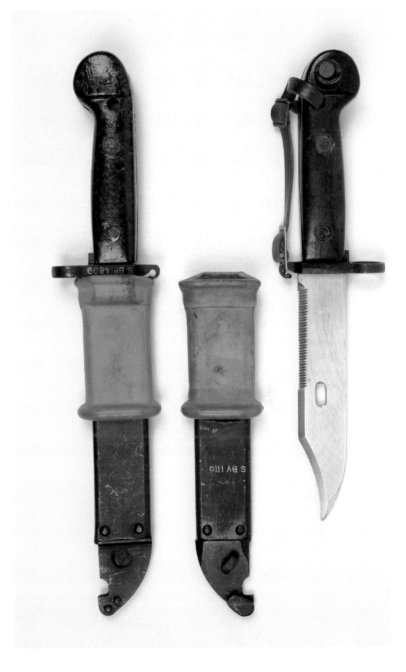

Most AK using nations had a short strap and carbine hook suspension for their bayonets. However, Romania adopted bayonet frogs for carriage. Shown here (left to right) are a black leather frog used by the Air Force, a brown leather frog and a leather and green web frog. (This web frog was found in Iraq, the pattern being standard issue for Iraqi troops.) Lithuania is also known to have used leather and web bayonet frogs on their Russian bayonets (for examples, see the Introduction). Media Image Photography

Romanian AKM I type bayonets. Romanian bayonets use a distinctive webbing or leather frog, so they lack the hanger arrangement typical of Russian AKM bayonets. The rubber scabbard grip section can be found in tan or grey, as shown here, and both bayonet and scabbard are usually adorned with a letter prefix serial number. Media Image Photography

Soviet Union (Russia)

The first Avtomat Kalashnikov assault rifle fielded by the Soviets had a stamped sheet metal receiver with a machined steel trunnion that fitted the barrel to the receiver. The receiver was produced in Type 1A with a fixed stock and Type 1B with a folding stock, the different stock requirements needing different rear faces to the receivers. The system of mass production employed for the Type 1 receiver resulted in excessive waste, particularly from the warping caused during welding. The Soviets were unable to overcome the problems, so in 1949 they reverted to the time-honoured method of machining the receiver from a forged block of steel. The lengthy machining process involved in producing the type 2 receiver reduced the weight of the original forged block from 2.7kg (6lb) to 635g (1.4lb). The outer forward end of the receiver had two machined areas, one at each side above the magazine well. These lightening recesses were milled parallel to the bore axis and serve to readily identify the forged and milled receiver type Kalashnikov from the earlier stamped receiver. The milled receiver was produced as type 2A fixed and 2B folding stock variants. The milled type 2 receiver worked well but the stock fixing was inadequate, often breaking or working loose, and thus needed modification. The steel extension block on the rear of the type 2 receiver, used to house the butt extension, was removed and the lower of the two steel tangs, which were screwed to the stock, was strengthened. An extension of the wooden stock fitted into a hollow at the rear of the receiver. To reduce stress on the butt the sling swivel was removed from the butt and moved to the rear left face of the receiver. The milled sections above the magazine well were also angled so that they now ran parallel to the lower edge of the receiver rather than the bore axis. The modified receiver, produced in fixed type A and folding type B from 1953, is known as the type 3 receiver by collectors, although in Russian military circles there was no distinction between the first three production receiver types, all of which were designated Avtomat Kalashnikov or AK.

While the type 3 receiver Kalashnikov proved to be a reliable and easy to use weapon, it was time-consuming and expensive to produce compared to the original, failed, type 1 receiver weapon. While the milled receiver weapon was being manufactured, Russian engineers had continued to work toward overcoming manufacturing problems and the production of a stamped receiver. Several prototype models were tested during the 1950s while production methods were refined and modernized. Eventually, in 1958, a stamped receiver Kalashnikov prototype met the requirements of the design and production teams. The following year a stamped receiver weapon was accepted into service as the Avtomat Kalashnikov Modernizirovanniy (AKM). Like the original type 1 receiver, the new type 4 stamped receiver AKM had machined steel trunnions to hold the barrel in the receiver and a rear trunnion to hold the stock. A number of improvements were incorporated, including a new receiver cover that used reinforcing ribs for strength and a newly designed knife bayonet. The AKM used extensive riveting and spot welding in its construction and resulted in a weapon that was some 1.1kg (2.5lb) lighter than the milled patterns. Surprisingly, the rear sight of the AKM was graduated to 1,000m (3,300ft) instead of the 800m (2,600ft) of the AK, although at such ranges the ballistic properties of the 7.62×39mm round would have produced little more than grazing fire.

Many years after the adoption of the 5.45×39mm AK74 as the Russian standard small arm, it is interesting to note that the Izhmash arsenal at Izhevsk is still advertising the standard 7.62×39mm AKM and AKMS rifle as available from stock.

During the early 1990s Izhmash introduced a new series of rifles called the AK100 series, chambered for a variety of common Russian and NATO calibre ammunition types. The AK74M (a modernized AK74 rifle with a side-folding full stock) provided the base for the new series of weapons that included the AK101, AK102, AK103, AK104 and AK105. Of these weapons the AK103 and the AK104 (a short barrel variant of the AK103) were both chambered for the 7.62×39mm cartridge. (As a calibre variant of the AK74 rifle, however, the type is not illustrated in this volume.)

The bayonet issued with the original AK was of a quite unusual design. The 56-X-212 or AK47 bayonet, as it is commonly called, was based on the earlier SVT 40 bayonet's blade and scabbard type with a new hilt design. The bayonet had a full muzzle ring that fitted over the muzzle nut and a second half ring or 'ears' on the upper pommel that fitted around the lower front end of the gas block. Although solid evidence is lacking, it is possible that the design was conceived as an afterthought, which would explain the novel design. The introduction of the AKM rifle saw the introduction of an innovative bayonet concept that would be copied by the British, and later the Americans, decades later. The 6X3 or AKM I bayonet had a plastic grip with bulbous pommel around the fixing mechanism. It had a standard crossguard (crosspiece) and muzzle ring, and a bowie or clip-point blade with a saw back, but void of fullers. A hole cut into the blade fitted over a post on the scabbard extension to form an effective wire-cutter. The scabbard had a narrow rubber grip section, often cited as electrical insulation. Its effectiveness as such, though, would undoubtedly have been impaired by the metal scabbard and crossguard, as the user would have found it difficult to avoid coming into contact with them when using the bayonet to cut any wire carrying an electric current. The wire-cutter was nonetheless quite efficient at defeating standard barbed and similar gauge wires. The pommel of the AKM I bayonet was prone to damage and the scabbard grip was inadequate. This led to the production of the 6X4 or AKM II bayonet. The AKM II bayonet used the same proven blade type with a new hilt with metal pommel and a new plastic-bodied scabbard. Scabbards were suspended from a leather belt loop using a spring clip that could easily be detached to allow the scabbard to be used for wire-cutting.

Both the AKM I and AKM II bayonets were fitted with a strap looped through the pommel and clipped to the crossguard. This leather or webbing strap looped over the back of the hand when the bayonet was used as a knife, helping prevent loss in hand-to-hand combat.

The earliest slings for the AK were made of a single length of webbing with a steel toothless buckle for adjustment, a leather retaining loop and a D ring and spring clip fitted at the free end using a leather tab. The leather tab was a weak point and subject to wear, leading to its replacement with a riveted steel end tab. For a period during the mid-1950s the sling was produced in leather. It is known that the leather sling was used by Soviet Naval infantry but nothing more is known of the reason for its production. The webbing pattern remained standard throughout the production period of the AK and AKM. The sling can be found with a leather, webbing or leatherette retaining loop

and in a variety of shades of tan colour, with some examples also being made in black and green.

Standard Variants

AK (AK47)	Type 1A stamped receiver, fixed stock
AKS (AKS47)	Type 1B stamped receiver, under-folding stock
AK (AK47)	Type 2A milled receiver, fixed stock
AKS (AKS47)	Type 2B milled receiver, under-folding stock
AK (AK47)	Type 3A milled receiver, fixed stock
AKS (AKS47)	Type 3B milled receiver, under-folding stock
AKM	Type 4A stamped receiver, fixed stock
AKMS	Type 4B stamped receiver, under-folding stock

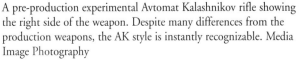

A pre-production experimental Avtomat Kalashnikov rifle showing the right side of the weapon. Despite many differences from the production weapons, the AK style is instantly recognizable. Media Image Photography

The pre-production experimental AK rifle, showing the left side of the weapon. Media Image Photography

The earliest production model of the Soviet Avtomat Kalashnikov rifle had a sheet steel receiver with an inset machined steel barrel trunnion, which is clearly visible below the cocking handle. This type of receiver is called the type 1 by collectors, although the Soviet authorities did not distinguish between the patterns. Weapon courtesy AJS Militaria

Left side of the type 1 receiver AK rifle, showing the markings on the trunnion. These consist of an individually hand-stamped serial number and date of manufacture, 1950. Weapon courtesy AJS Militaria

The second generation of AK rifles used a milled steel receiver. The type 2 receiver featured distinct milled depressions on both sides, above the magazine well, and a distinct trunnion protrusion visible below the cocking handle. The AK type 2 is readily recognizable by the steel extension at the rear of the receiver, which was used to fix the wooden stock to the receiver. The weapon used the same sling fixing points as the AK type 1, at the front of the fore-end and on the wooden stock. Weapon courtesy Antiques Storehouse

Type 2 milled receiver AK showing the milled section, parallel to the axis of the rifle bore. The markings comprise an Izhmash triangle arrow logo, the date (1953) and the weapon serial number. Weapon courtesy Antiques Storehouse

Soviet soldiers carry the type 2 milled receiver AK at the Soviet war memorial in the western sector of divided Berlin, May 1959. At the time the Soviets were putting pressure on the western powers to pull out of the city. Private collection.

The third type of receiver used on the AK rifle was an improved version of the type 2 designed to overcome problems that had been encountered with the fitting of the stock to the receiver. On the type 3 receiver AK the forward sling attachment was moved to a position on the gas block and the rear swivel was relocated to the receiver. Media Image Photography

Type 3 AK receiver markings, showing the Izhmash arrow mark and the weapon serial number. The milled sections at either side of the magazine housing are cut parallel with the lower edge of the receiver, giving them a sloped appearance. Media Image Photography

Right side of the type 3 AK receiver showing the selector markings. The selector is set at safe in this image with a Cyrillic 'AV' for Avtomatichiskiy (full auto) and 'OD' Odinochniy (single shot). Media Image Photography

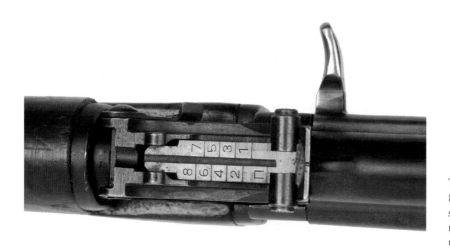

Type 3 milled receiver AK sight ranged to 800m with a Cyrillic 'P' for the battle sight setting. All of the early AK rifles were ranged to 800m: given the type of sights used and the relatively short sight base, however, this was somewhat optimistic. Media Image Photography

Detail of the foresight block of the type 3 milled receiver AK, showing the removable barrel nut and the muzzle nut lock (a small plunger at the top edge of the nut). The round section at the upper section of the block is the foresight stud, which can be moved left or right to adjust windage for zero. Media Image Photography

Soviet- made supplementary night sight shown fitted to the foresight post of an AK rifle. The luminous bead fitted over the foresight but could be slid down the wire fitting spring for daytime use. Media Image Photography

The wooden pistol grip of the type 3 receiver AK rifle. This example has a very fine chequered finish. Also shown is the rear sling swivel, moved to the receiver on the type 3 AK. On the type 1 and 2 receiver AK the swivel had been mounted on the wooden stock. Media Image Photography

Afghan National Police officers armed with Kalashnikov rifles: (left) a type 3 receiver Russian AK and (right) a Romanian PM md 65. Kandahar province, Afghanistan, 2011. US Department of Defense

The fourth receiver type produced for the Kalashnikov rifle saw the successful introduction in 1959 of a stamped sheet steel pattern, and a change in nomenclature to AKM (Avtomat Kalashnikova Modernizirovanniy). Media Image Photography

Right side of the AKM receiver showing the modified selector lever with added central reinforcing rib. The receiver of the AKM was fitted with a selector stop to prevent the lever being forced down too far; it is positioned at the forward edge of the trigger guard. The selector in this image is set at Avtomatichiskiy (full auto). Media Image Photography

Left side of the AKM showing the Izhmash arrow logo, the date of manufacture (1974) and the weapon serial number stamped into the barrel trunnion. The last three digits, '910', are also marked on the receiver cover, which was made of thinner steel than that used on the AK. In order to strengthen it, a series of ribs were stamped into the sheet metal. Media Image Photography

The barrel and sight block of the AKM rifle. The muzzle nut common to the AK variants was replaced by an angled muzzle brake that helped reduce muzzle climb when the weapon was fired in full automatic. The AKM muzzle brake can be found retrospectively fitted to AK rifles. The sight block was reduced in width to help decrease the weight of the AKM. Media Image Photography

Russian AKM rifle plastic pistol grip with moulded diamond hatching to improve hold. Media Image Photography

Soviet AKM rifle in use with Indonesian troops. The Indonesians also used the AK rifle, for which they manufactured their own bayonet with cross-hatched black plastic grips (see Introduction). US Department of Defense

The folding stock variant of the AKM was called the AKMS (Avtomat Kalashnikova Modernizirovanniy Skladnoy). The stamped folding stock is reinforced with impressed ridges and steel strips riveted on the internal face. This example has a muzzle nut fitted rather than the usual muzzle brake of the AKM series. Media Image Photography

Rear sight of the AKMS showing the graduations to 1,000m, with the battle sight marked by a Cyrillic 'P'. The effective range of the weapon was probably closer to 300m, with 1,000m being little more than harassing fire. Media Image Photography

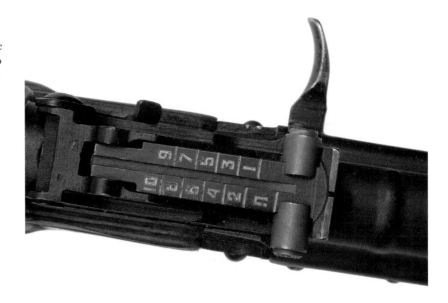

Detail of the AKMS barrel and sight block. This example has been fitted with a muzzle nut rather than the usual muzzle brake. Media Image Photography

Left receiver of a 1965 dated AKM manufactured at Izhmash. The rivet points for the trunnion and circular weld marks for the internal bolt guide are clearly evident, as is the depression above the magazine housing that acts as a magazine guide. Media Image Photography

The wooden AK style pistol grip of the AKMS rifle. Also shown is the release button for the folding stock. The grey bolt set in a stamped reinforcing 'V' is the trigger pin, while the dome-headed rivets secure the back plate (also called the rear trunnion) that reinforces the receiver and holds the stock secure. Media Image Photography

US Marines on exercise in Mongolia are instructed in the use of the Kalashnikov rifle used by Mongolian forces. The Mongolian Ranger Captain is using a Russian-made AKMS for this demonstration. US Department of Defense

Detail of the folding stock fitted to the Russian AKMS rifle. Media Image Photography

A Soviet GP25 40mm grenade launcher
fitted to an AKM rifle. The GP25 is a
muzzle-loading launcher designed for the
AK74. Copies were produced by a number
of nations. The GP25 and its successor, the
GP30, have been retrospectively fitted to
AK and AKM rifles by nations not
equipped with the AK74. Western forces
only became aware of the GP25's existence
when Soviet troops were observed using
the launcher in Afghanistan. It is shown
here in use by an Afghan soldier during
2008, the right side of the launcher being
visible on the AKM. Canadian Forces
DND CFJIC AR2008-K124-27

Although rather poor in quality, this image
from a 1960s US military intelligence
manual on the AK rifle shows a rare cup
type grenade discharger unit fitted to the
barrel of an AK rifle. Little is known about
the production of this item and no other
images have been seen by the author. This
style was common during World War I. It
would probably have been used with the
F1 offensive hand grenade and a Ballistite
grenade-launching cartridge. It was
replaced by the simple tubular pattern of
launcher that screwed to the barrel in place
of the barrel nut (for details of this grenade
launcher attachment, see Yugoslavia
below). US Department of Defense

Afghanistan, August 2010. An Afghan National Police officer armed with an AKM rifle with a Russian GP style launcher fitted in somewhat of a 'jury rig'. The launcher is held to the AKM by the use of two large hose clamps. US Department of Defense

Protective cover or 'drop bag' designed to hold the AKS or AKMS with the stock folded. Cut-outs in the cover allowed the sling to be used while the weapon was still inside. Media Image Photography

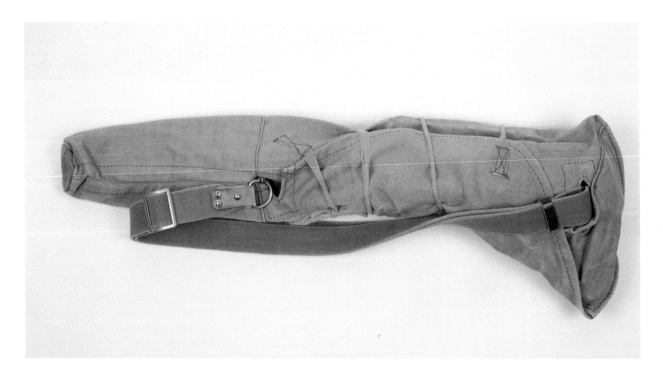

Typical Soviet manufacture AK slings. Fitted to a type 3 receiver AK is a 1951 dated webbing sling with leather end tab. On the type 3 receiver the sling attachment points were moved from the front of the fore-end to the gas block and from the wood stock to the rear of the receiver. Laid out below is a 1955 dated brown leather sling fitted with the stronger steel end tab holding the D ring and carbine clip; a web sling with web slider; and, bottom, a web sling with leather slider. Media Image Photography

Typical Soviet production three-pocket ammunition pouch for 30-round magazines. The two external pockets hold the dual oil and cleaning solution container and the combination tool (shown at right), along with three 30-round plastic magazines and two 7.62×39mm ball rounds. Each soldier would carry four magazines – three in the pouch and one on the weapon – giving him a total of 120 rounds of ammunition. Also shown are two 7.62×39mm ball rounds. Media Image Photography

Tension on the Sino-Soviet border, Kamennaya, 1969. A Soviet Leytenánt (Lieutenant) makes a report via field telephone while the soldier alongside him takes aim with his AKM. This view clearly shows the standard magazine pouch worn on the soldier's belt. Private collection

Typical magazine types used with AK rifles (left to right): early slab-sided magazine; standard ribbed magazine; ribbed magazine with Izhmash arrow below the central rib; red plastic magazine. The plastic magazine weighed only 170g (6oz) compared to the 330g (11.6oz) of the steel magazine. Media Image Photography

Illustration from a 1972 Soviet field manual showing the 'PBS' sound suppressor (silencer) for the AKM and AKMS rifles. The suppressor required special subsonic ammunition and a special rear sight calibrated for both the standard ball and the low-powered suppressor ammunition. Above is the PBS fitted to an AKM rifle, below is the PBS-1 suppressor disassembled. Media Image Photography

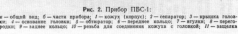

Izhevsk manufactured knife bayonet for the Avtomat Kalashnikov fitted to a type 3 receiver AK. This type of bayonet is generally referred to as the AK47 bayonet by collectors. The original Soviet factory designation was 56-X-212, although in period manuals it is generally only referred to as the AK bayonet. Media Image Photography

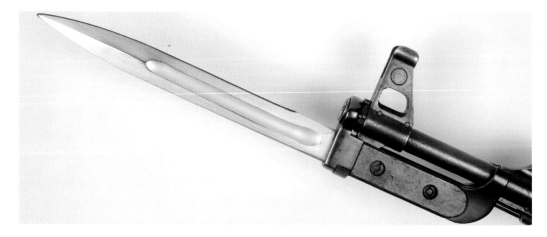

Detail of the crossguard marking of an AK bayonet, showing the small Izhevsk arrow and triangle manufacturer's mark. Media Image Photography

Soviet-made bayonets for the AKM rifles. At left is the original AKM bayonet, designated the 6X3 but often called the AKM I by collectors. It is readily identifiable by its bulbous pommel and rubber sleeve on the scabbard. Centre is the intermediate AKM bayonet, comprising the AKM I bayonet mated with a later production Izhevsk-marked AKM II scabbard, an officially sanctioned variant. At right is the 6X4 or AKM II bayonet with metal pommel and new scabbard. The AKM II was developed because of a tendency for the plastic pommel of the AKM I to become damaged in use. This bayonet introduced a wire-cutter plate at the scabbard tip. When married to the blade notch, the combination produced a scissor-type wire-cutter. Media Image Photography

Detail of the Tula factory star marking on the rear of an AKM II scabbard. Media Image Photography

Yugoslavia (Serbia)

The communist-governed Federal People's Republic of Yugoslavia, formed in 1945, declared itself a neutral nation only three years later, with allegiance to neither the Eastern nor Western forces (later Warsaw Pact and NATO). The first weapon produced was the M48 rifle, a close copy of the German K98. This was later replaced by a Yugoslav-made improved version of the Russian SKS rifle, the M59, which differed only in detail from the SKS. The M59 was soon upgraded to the M59/66, which had a permanently attached grenade launcher. The additional length of the launcher necessitated the use of a much longer bayonet than on the standard SKS.

In 1964 Yugoslavia began licensed production of the AK rifle. The Yugoslav M64 rifle (Automatska Puska 64) had the standard AK milled section on the right side of the receiver but it was not present on the left side, which had a distinctive raised step. The M64 was unique in having a C.500mm barrel (as opposed to the C.415mm AK standard). The M64A incorporated a grenade launcher sight on the gas block that operated a gas cut-off when in the raised position. The cut-off prevented the combustion gases being channelled from the barrel to the piston, allowing the full force of the cartridge propellant to be used to launch the grenade, rather than re-cycle the weapon's action. The M64B was the folding stock version and used the Russian pattern of under-folding stock. To aid in absorbing recoil shock from grenade launching, the wooden stock M64A rifle is fitted with an integral rubber butt. However, the recoil from grenade launching could dislodge the receiver cover. To prevent loss of the cover the M64A and M64B rifles had a small spring-loaded bolt that locked the recoil spring guide in place, thus serving to preventing the receiver cover being dislodged. The weapons were also fitted with a bolt 'hold open' device that held the bolt back after the last round had been fired. In 1970 the Yugoslav authorities introduced a modified version of the M64, the M70. The new weapon was similar to the M64 and had a milled section on the right of the receiver but the left side of the receiver was flat. The bolt 'hold open' was removed from the new weapon. Instead, the magazine's follower plate had a distinct flat to the rear edge, the flat serving to hold back the bolt after the last round was fired (the standard Soviet magazine pattern allowed the bolt to slide over the empty magazines carrier). The folding stock variant was called the M70A with the fixed stock being the M70. Neither the M64 nor the M70 variants were produced in great numbers.

Soon after the adoption of the M70 Yugoslavia began production of the stamped receiver AKM design. The stamped receiver weapons were designated the M70B1 for the fixed stock version and M70AB2 for the folding stock variant. The new weapons incorporated the grenade launcher sight and night sights of the earlier Yugoslav models, but the receivers were made of 1.5mm steel as opposed to the 1mm that was standard on AKM production. The barrel trunnion used on the M70B1 and M70AB2 was not the standard AKM type. The Yugoslavs adopted the sturdier pattern as used on the RPK light machine gun. This gave the M70B1 and M70AB2 rifles distinctive trunnion bulges on either side of the forward receiver to accommodate the larger RPK type trunnion.

The fore-ends and handguards of Yugoslav weapons have three vent holes in the woodwork: with the exception of Iraq, other nations' fore-ends and handguards used only two vents as standard. All Yugoslav AK types also used the smooth receiver cover. As with the Iraqi Tabuk rifles, Yugoslav handguards, fore-ends and receiver covers were not interchangeable with those of the standard AK or AKM. Similarly the rear sight was also set back, giving the Yugoslav weapons a longer sight base of 393mm.

It is believed that Yugoslavia did not produce an AK47 or an AKM I type bayonet: neither pattern of obvious Yugoslav manufacture has been observed by the author. With the adoption of the M70B1 and M70AB2 stamped receiver weapons the Yugoslavs introduced an AKM II type bayonet. A copy of the standard Soviet AKM II, it had a polished blade with a black finish to the metalwork with black plastic grips and scabbard body. The scabbard hanger was of brown leather.

Yugoslavia did not use the Russian style rifle slings for its M70 rifles but instead produced its own design. The Yugoslav sling consisted of a single length of webbing with a reinforcing tab at the free end and a flat steel hook stitched at the opposite end. The design of hook required a much broader fitting on the gas block than was usual with Russian or other weapons. Adjustment was by means of a free-running toothless buckle.

Standard Variants

M64	Milled receiver, fixed stock. Long 500mm barrel
M64A	Milled receiver, fixed stock
M64B	Milled receiver, under-folding stock
M70	Milled receiver, fixed stock
M70A	Milled receiver, under-folding stock
M70A1	Milled receiver, under-folding stock. Mounting bracket for optical sights
M70B1	Stamped receiver, fixed stock
M70AB2	Stamped receiver, under-folding stock
M70B1N	Stamped receiver, fixed stock. Mounting bracket for optical sights
M70AB2N	Stamped receiver, under-folding stock. Mounting bracket for optical sights

An Afghan soldier using a Yugoslavian milled receiver folding stock M70A rifle during training. The soldier is manually ejecting the blank ammunition spent cases as there is no blank firing adaptor attached to the weapon and thus the action would fail to cycle. The M70's serial number was engraved in the milled section above the magazine well rather than on the barrel trunnion. Both the front and rear integral night sights are raised on this weapon. US Department of Defense

An early 1970s photograph of a JNA (Yugoslav National Army) soldier preparing to fire a TKM M60 rifle grenade from his Automatska Puska M64A milled receiver rifle. The M64A was the grenade launcher version of the M64 and was later renamed the M70A. Only the right side of the receiver has the milled-out section above the magazine well. He carries the canvas five-magazine shoulder-slung pouch at his right side. Early variants of the pouch were made of leather. Private collection

Yugoslav milled receiver folding-stock M70A rifle in use with the ANA. This view clearly shows the left side of the receiver is lacking the milled section usually found on type 2 and type 3 AK receivers. Also present is the factory logo and marking 'ZASTAVA-KRAGUJEVAC YUGOSLAVIA'. US Department of Defense

The Yugoslav M70B1 rifle was a fixed-stock, grenade-launching rifle based on the AKM. The M70B1 used an RPK LMG type barrel trunnion that required the receiver to have the distinctive bulge visible below the cocking handle. The grenade launcher is not fitted on this example. This weapon is fitted with a Soviet plastic magazine that bears Serbian graffiti. Media Image Photography

Detail of the left side of the M70B1 showing the distinctive bulge below the barrel trunnion markings. The trunnion bears the manufacturer's mark 'ZASTAVA-KRAGUJEVAC YUGOSLAVIA', the serial number and the date of manufacture, 1984. Media Image Photography

M70B1 lock for the recoil spring guide. The small button needs to be depressed before the spring guide catch can be depressed to release the receiver cover. This prevents the cover from being dislodged when firing grenades. On Yugoslav weapons the rear sling swivel was fitted on the rear of the receiver on both milled and stamped receiver types. Media Image Photography

The M70AB2 was the folding-stock version of the M70B1. It had an under-folding stock and like the M70B1 it had grenade-launching sights, a detachable grenade launcher and integral night sights. The grenade launcher is fitted to this example, with the muzzle nut stored on the cleaning rod. Media Image Photography

M70AB2 rifle with the stock folded under against the receiver. The night sights are both raised on this weapon, which is fitted with a standard Yugoslav production magazine. Media Image Photography

The M70AB2 rifle's folding stock shown in the open position. Media Image Photography

Detail of the left side of the M70AB2 receiver showing the date of manufacture as 1992, the designation M70AB2 and the weapon's serial number. This weapon does not have the Zastava manufacturer's mark. Media Image Photography

M70AB2 selector lever and markings. Safe is represented by a letter 'U' (Ukeceno), single shot is marked by an 'R' (Rafalna) and automatic is shown by a 'J' (Jedinacna). When closed the under-folding stock interfered with the use of the selector lever. This was partially overcome by the use of a modified selector lever with a small tab at the top rear edge of the selector, accessible when the stock was folded, in addition to the one at the lower front edge. This simple yet effective modification was also used on Iraqi Tabuk under-folding stock weapons. Media Image Photography

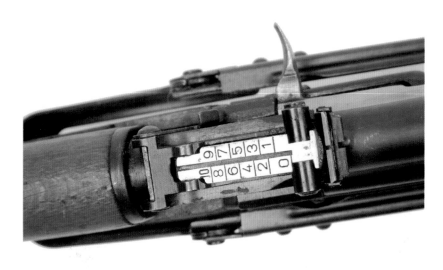

M70AB2 rear sight graduated to 1,000m, with the battle sight position shown by a '0'. Media Image Photography

The foresight post and night sight in the raised position on an M70AB2. The grenade launcher is fitted to the weapon's muzzle. Media Image Photography

An M70AB2 rifle rear sight with the flip-up night sight in the raised position. The same sights were fitted on the M70B1. Media Image Photography

The pistol grip used on Yugoslav weapons was made from black plastic that had horizontal ribs for improved grip. This is the grip fitted to an M70AB2 rifle. Media Image Photography

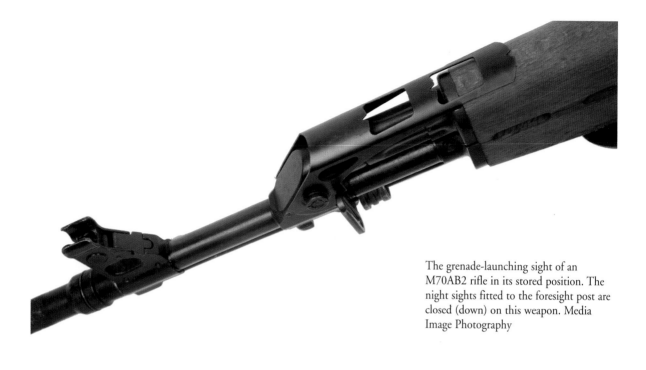

The grenade-launching sight of an M70AB2 rifle in its stored position. The night sights fitted to the foresight post are closed (down) on this weapon. Media Image Photography

The grenade launcher tube and the launching sight in the raised firing position on an M70AB2 rifle. Raising the sight cuts off the gas flow to the piston, allowing all the propellant gases to be used to launch the grenade. Media Image Photography

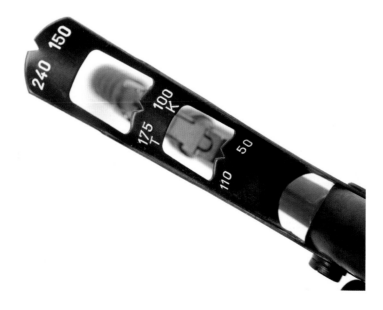

M70AB2 grenade-launching sight. The left side is graduated at 110, 175T (Trenutna) and 240m. These graduations are for use when using the TTM M60 HE anti-personnel rifle grenade. The right side is graduated at 50, 100K (Kumulativna) and 150m for the heavier TKM M60 HE shaped charge anti-tank rifle grenade. Media Image Photography

Using a tree for cover and support, a Serbian army soldier takes aim with his folding stock M70AB2 rifle. Republic of Serbia Ministry of Defence

Yugoslav BTKM M68 practice grenade fitted to the launcher of an M70AB2 rifle. The BTKM M68 replicated the ballistic performance of the TKM M60 HE shaped charge anti-tank rifle grenade. This particular example was found in Iraq. All Yugoslav rifle grenades were issued with a grenade-launching cartridge stored in the hollow of the tail section as standard ball ammunition could not be used. Media Image Photography

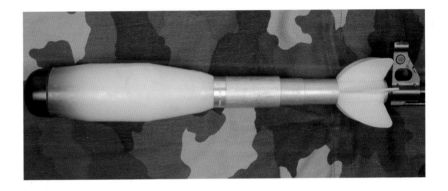

A case of grenades found at the Serbian Special Police Station in Brcko, Bosnia-Herzegovina, during 1997. The haul includes TKM M60 and TTM M60 anti-personnel rifle grenades, M62 smoke rifle grenades and M79 anti-tank hand grenades. US Department of Defense

Yugoslav M70 type slings. Fitted to an M70B1 (with Yugoslav pattern magazine attached) is the standard green webbing sling. Laid below is an early khaki version of the M70 sling. Media Image Photography

Yugoslav and Serbian four-pocket 30-round AK magazine pouches (left to right): original JNA pattern leather pouch; second pattern canvas pouch with Yugoslav pattern AK magazine; Serbian 1990s camouflage pouch. All of the pouches have a shoulder strap and belt fitting on the rear. Media Image Photography

Serbian single-pocket hard shell magazine pouches in plain green and camouflage pattern. This type of pouch was produced in both left and right variants and was used with the M98 ballistic vest and M99 tactical vest. At right is a black soft shell pouch used by police units and a Yugoslav-made 20-round capacity M70 magazine. Media Image Photography

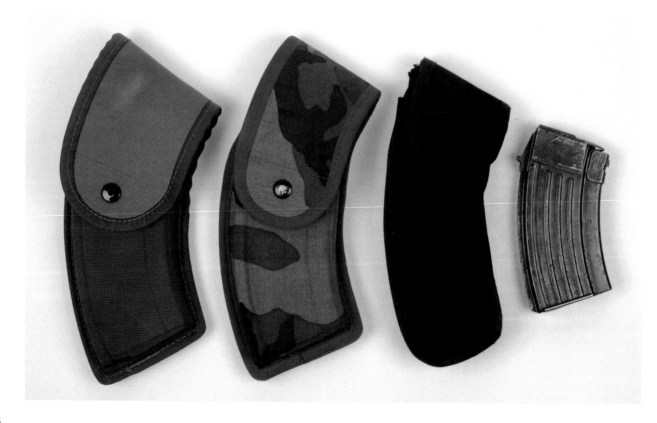

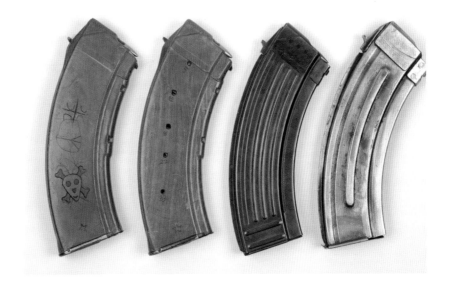

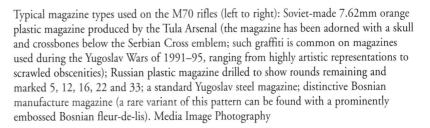

Typical magazine types used on the M70 rifles (left to right): Soviet-made 7.62mm orange plastic magazine produced by the Tula Arsenal (the magazine has been adorned with a skull and crossbones below the Serbian Cross emblem; such graffiti is common on magazines used during the Yugoslav Wars of 1991–95, ranging from highly artistic representations to scrawled obscenities); Russian plastic magazine drilled to show rounds remaining and marked 5, 12, 16, 22 and 33; a standard Yugoslav steel magazine; distinctive Bosnian manufacture magazine (a rare variant of this pattern can be found with a prominently embossed Bosnian fleur-de-lis). Media Image Photography

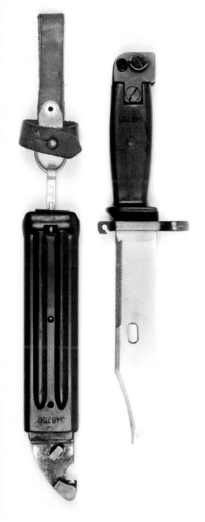

Yugoslav M70 bayonet. Yugoslavia produced only an AKM Type II bayonet for use with its M70 series of rifles. While similar to the East German AKM II, they differ in having a brown leather hanger and other minor details, including the design of the press catch and the shape of the pommel. Media Image Photography

Serbian troops, serving with the United Nations, parade with M70 bayonets fixed to their M70AB2 rifles. Republic of Serbia Ministry of Defence

Index